Teaching Orientation and Mobility in the Schools

An Instructor's Companion

Natalie Isaak Knott

AFB PRESS
American Foundation for the Blind

Library of Congress Cataloging-in-Publication Data

Knott, Natalie Isaak.
    Teaching orientation and mobility in the schools : an instructor's companion / Natalie Isaak Knott.
       p. cm.
    Includes bibliographical references and index.
    ISBN 0-89128-391-9
    1. Children, Blind—Orientation and mobility—Study and teaching. 2. Children with visual disabilities—Orientation and mobility—Study and teaching. 3. Orientation and mobility instructors. I. Title.
    HV1596.5 .K56 2002
    362.4′1′083—dc21   2002025592

All photographs by Natalie Isaak Knott

The American Foundation for the Blind—the organization to which Helen Keller devoted more than 40 years of her life—is a national nonprofit whose mission is to eliminate the inequities faced by the ten million Americans who are blind or visually impaired. Headquartered in New York City, AFB maintains offices in Atlanta, Chicago, Dallas, San Francisco, and a governmental relations office in Washington, DC.

It is the policy of the American Foundation for the Blind to use in the first printing of its books acid-free paper that meet the ANSI Z39.48 Standard. The infinity symbol that appears above indicates that the paper in this printing meets that standard.

Contents

Introduction

The inspiration for this book grew from my experience, not only as a teacher struggling to find answers for myself, but as a master teacher to orientation and mobility (O&M) student teachers and as a mentor to independent O&M contractors working in the school district where I am employed. By and large, these were people who were teaching children and adolescents in a public school setting for the first time and were encountering an array of unique challenges. I envisioned a handbook of guidelines to present to them, one that would help to fill the gap between the underlying theories upon which the teaching of O&M is based and the substance of daily practice.

The need for such an "instructor's companion" became even more marked after the 1997 reauthorization of the Individuals with Disabilities Education Act (IDEA) designated O&M as a "related service," one that schools are required to provide for their students, giving it a more central role in the education of visually impaired children. Indeed, some O&M instructors who are trained to work with adults may find themselves working with young people and children in schools. This book is for them as well.

The result, *Teaching Orientation and Mobility in the Schools,* was "written" in schools, streets, and communities and reflects the struggles involved in teaching but, more important, its concomitant, the struggle of students to learn *and* their ultimate victories. It was also written with the conviction that the student belongs at the heart of the teaching process as the primary subject, rather than the object.

This book describes a path from the pile of books and papers, which marks the end of formal O&M instruction at the university, to the safe street crossing of a girl who is blind and has multiple disabilities to the independent bus trip of an apprehensive 13-year-old boy with low vision. It reflects the metamorphosis of theory into practice, in which the letter of theory blends with the spirit of practice to become something fluid and unique, something functional, adapted, often approximate, and rarely perfect.

Thus, the choice of topics addressed in this book was derived from the issues and questions that arose in my own learning process and that of my student teachers and colleagues and from the issues that consistently surface as we work with our students. It is intended not as a comprehensive O&M manual—university texts exist for that purpose—but as a manual based on the practical experience of seasoned mentors passed on to newer teachers in the field.

The material that follows is intended to indicate approaches to teaching and to supply examples of forms and processes that may be used directly or as a springboard for the reader's creativity. I hope that this book will provide information and guidance to facilitate a newcomer's entrance into the often-confusing realm of the public schools and will provide more experienced practitioners with fresh ideas and approaches to consider. Above all, it is my hope that this work will give insights into and support for the joyous challenge of teaching O&M to young people.

Overview

When an orientation and mobility (O&M) specialist begins to work in a public school system, he or she assumes a demanding job with many and diverse responsibilities. In addition, an O&M specialist works for the most part independently, apart from the advice and support that everyday interaction with coworkers may offer. In some ways, therefore, this book is intended to serve the role of a friendly colleague to provide some of the information and suggestions that an experienced coworker may contribute. But before plunging into the details of the O&M specialist's work, this chapter offers an overview of the nature and responsibilities that are fundamental to the position of O&M specialist in the public schools and explains its legal underpinnings.

ROLE AND RESPONSIBILITY OF THE O&M SPECIALIST

O&M specialists are employed by public school districts to provide specialized instructional services to a specific population of students who are visually impaired or blind as part of an educational team of professionals who serve these students in different capacities. They teach "pullout" classes—in which specific students are pulled out of their regular classrooms—as opposed to teaching all students in a classroom as general education teachers do. These pullout classes consist primarily of students who are served singly and in a serial fashion throughout the day. There may be only one O&M student in a school, so the O&M specialist may visit a number of schools in a day or week in the process of serving his or her caseload.

The frequency and times of services allotted to each student are determined by an assessment of the student's needs and abilities and then documented in the student's Individualized Education Program (IEP), which is a written plan of instruction (see Chapter 4). (The plan for children under age 3 is known as an Individualized Family Service Plan, and for students after age 14, a transition plan must also be written.) Different students require different levels of services, so caseloads vary, depending on the students' needs. For example, the O&M specialist may meet with students three times a week for an hour each time, one hour per week, or half an hour twice a week. At times, students may have two- to three-hour lessons to learn extended community travel. Some students are monitored only periodically.

O&M specialists usually work closely with their students and get to know them well because of the usual one-on-one nature of the position. They may also work closely with the students' parents at times. In addition, they spend some of their scheduled work time doing assessments, conducting observations, processing referrals, preparing lessons and materials, ordering materials, evaluating sites and travel routes, writing reports and correspondence, keeping records, attending meetings, consulting with other professionals, making phone calls, and driving from site to site.

Itinerant Status

Because of the low incidence of students who are visually impaired or blind, as well as the practices of mainstreaming, full inclusion, and placement of students with disabilities in neighborhood schools, there may be only one visually impaired student at a given school. Thus, the service mode for O&M teaching in the public schools is primarily itinerant, with one-on-one instruction. O&M specialists are traveling teachers. At best, they are ambassadors, and at worst, strangers in a strange land. Their teaching domain is limited only by the natural geographic features of their areas and the constraints of time and common sense. In the course of a single day, the teacher may go to the park with a preschooler, work on the logistics of mainstreaming a kindergartner, travel with a student to shop at a supermarket, and work with still another student on combined travel by bus and a rapid transit system to a neighboring city. In the process of carrying out diverse duties to a varied population in a variety of settings, it is important to adhere to professional organizational practices that support the integrity and effectiveness of one's work as a teacher.

Typical Responsibilities

O&M specialists are responsible for determining whether visually impaired students who have been referred for evaluation need O&M training and, if so, what kind. To do so they conduct observations and assessments of students; read students' records; and consult with other school personnel, parents, and medical specialists. When it is established that a student requires O&M services, they write a section of the IEP with appropriate goals and objectives for O&M skills and techniques.

O&M specialists then provide services directly, usually working one on one with students and occasionally with small groups. They also provide indirect services for students who do not receive direct O&M services, but have O&M goals infused into their daily program, to be worked on by their classroom teacher and possibly paraeducators or teaching assistants. O&M specialists will monitor these students in a variety of settings and provide consultation and modeling for other staff and parents regarding the students' needs and the best ways to work with him. O&M specialists also instruct parents and other family members, administrators, community members, teachers, and the classmates of O&M students by conducting training sessions to increase their understanding of the students' disabilities and means of working with them. These sessions may involve creating hands-on simulation experiences in which the participants wear vision occluders and are introduced to the challenges of traveling with limited or no vision while using assorted techniques and travel aids. The job may also include conducting environmental assessments of students' homes, schools, or communities and consulting with other professionals.

The majority of O&M instruction takes place out of the classroom, involves much walking, and extends throughout the school and into the community. Driving from school to school is a significant part of the job, as is transporting the students by vehicle, taking public transportation, or walking with them to a variety of sites in the community. Students are taught to travel safely, efficiently, and confidently using their remaining vision, if any, and other senses and special devices, such as long canes and monocular telescopes. To support lessons, the O&M specialist is responsible for lesson planning and creating a variety of materials, including large-print and tactile maps. The O&M specialist may also work with a braille transcriber or media specialist to create braille and other types of learning materials.

Because of the itinerant nature of the job, O&M specialists have unique schedules that may vary from day to day. They are not tied strictly to the regular bell schedule of a single site like a classroom teacher, but may be responsible for setting up their own daily schedules. In addition, they have a variety of "bosses" beyond their special education supervisors, depending on the administrative territory within which they are working, including the principals at each site where they serve students and a variety of administrators within the special education hierarchy.

Despite the nomadic nature of the O&M specialist's position, it is usually moored to the school district's special services department and specifically to the program for students with visual impairments, if there is one. It is here that O&M specialists may find peers in other teachers who work with students with visual impairments. Depending on the size and organization of the program, there may be staff meetings to attend that deal with all the details of providing services and maintaining the program for students with visual impairments.

Varied Subjects

The O&M specialist can anticipate teaching a wide variety of mainly nonacademic skills, all of which ultimately contribute to a student's increased ability to travel independently in a world designed for people with sight. Such skills range from the identification of body parts and their movements to the execution of an independent trip on public transportation, from traveling with a cane to using a pay phone, from reading a board menu with a monocular telescope to using a tactile map to plan a trip, and from identifying the texture of carpeting to interpreting wind currents in a hallway.

Diverse Caseloads

In the public schools, the ages and abilities of the students in an O&M specialist's caseload can be extremely varied. The students may include infants in early intervention programs run by a school district's special education division; elementary, middle, and secondary school-aged students in regular and special classes; and young adults up to age 22 in special transition classes. The students may have widely varying degrees of visual impairments, ranging from low vision to total blindness. Their cognitive abilities may also differ, as may their ambulatory abilities; some may use quad canes, walkers, or wheelchairs to facilitate travel. Some students may have one disability, and others may have multiple disabilities. However, all students in the caseload have one thing in common: They are all blind or visually impaired.

Supporting Documents and Procedures

With such complex and varied responsibilities, the O&M specialist who works in the public schools processes, organizes, and is accountable for a great deal of information. This information can become a powerful resource when consistent procedures and appropriate support documents are used. Organized information and procedures promote efficiency and make the job less stressful, thereby freeing energy for the task of teaching. Many documents, forms, and procedures are presented in this book as examples of ways to organize information that is collected about students. These documents may be used as presented or adapted to fit individual needs.

Personal Attributes

The process of teaching O&M both requires and encourages the growth of the personal qualities of resourcefulness, endurance, imagination, creativity, flexibility, patience, a sense of humor, and an abiding concern for people. The O&M specialist's classroom is one without desks, walls, or a ceiling. It expands and contracts according to the scope of the students' abilities and skills. Because of this lack of customary boundaries, the O&M specialist and student can encounter a wide variety of changing and unpredictable experiences, including the weather, traffic conditions, and other people's attitudes. The O&M specialist is responsible for creating structure where there appears to be none. He or she strives to help the students distill meaning from the chaos of sensory stimuli that surrounds them so their understanding of the world and how to get around in it may grow.

LEGAL FOUNDATIONS FOR PROVIDING O&M SERVICES

O&M is the profession that teaches persons who are blind or visually impaired the crucial skills needed to travel independently and safely. It assists in the development of orientation skills and safe movement, both indoors and out, in a student's home, school, and community. As a recent policy statement from the Office of Special Education and Rehabilitative Services (2000) of the U.S. Department of Education noted:

> For some blind and visually impaired children, the inability to move around independently can be a formidable obstacle to participating in school, family, and community life. . . . Acquisition of orientation and mobility skills, like the acquisition of other skills such as academic and social skills, is of great importance to the social and economic independence of blind and visually impaired persons.

Despite their importance to people who are blind or visually impaired, not every student who needs O&M services always receives them. It is crucial to understand, therefore, that these services are guaranteed by law. For the first time, the 1997 amendments to the Individuals with Disabilities Education Act (IDEA)—the legislation that governs the education of children with disabilities—designate O&M as one of the "related services" that may be required to assist a child who is blind or visually impaired to benefit from special education. This legislation thus makes explicit the inclusion of O&M among the range of services to be provided within the framework of the public schools. Guidelines for interpreting the law require that the delivery of O&M services be conducted by trained and knowledgeable personnel who meet appropriate state qualification standards.

Even with the legal mandates for services, however, there are potential obstacles to a student's receiving O&M services from a school district in an appropriate and timely manner. These obstacles may include selection criteria for services that exclude students who are less severely visually impaired or have multiple handicaps; the lack of available O&M specialists; limited financial resources; time restrictions; increased paperwork; liability concerns that might prevent a student from being taken off campus; and the trend toward provision of generic services by teachers who may have no vision or O&M training (Crouse & Bina, 1997). It is crucial that O&M specialists understand the right of each student with disabilities to assessment and appropriate services, including O&M services, so they can work to ensure that their students receive the services to which they are entitled.

IDEA

The Individuals with Disabilities Education Act (IDEA, previously known as P.L. 94-142, or the Education for all Handicapped Children Act of 1975), is the basic federal legislation governing the provision of educational services in the United States to children with disabilities. IDEA mandates that public schools provide to all eligible children with disabilities a free, appropriate public education in the least restrictive environment that is appropriate to each individual. The concept of least restrictive environment is a major tenet of IDEA, indicating that students must be integrated with their nondisabled peers to the greatest degree possible. IDEA requires that all public school systems develop appropriate IEPs that spell out the educational goals and objectives and the special services required for each child. The specific special education and related services that are delineated in each child's IEP must reflect the unique needs of that child. As noted, the regulations interpreting the 1997 revision of IDEA, adopted in March 1999, include orientation and mobility, as a body of services, as a "related service" that is required, as appropriate, to be provided to children who are visually impaired or blind.

Guidelines for Services

The National Association of State Directors of Special Education (in cooperation with the Hilton/Perkins Program), acting in an advocacy role for students with low-incidence disabilities, developed and published a set of guidelines for high-quality programs that serve students with visual impairments (Pugh & Erin, 1999). Among its detailed recommendations, *Blind and Visually Impaired Students: Educational Service Guidelines* further outlines the need for O&M services and O&M service providers and includes guidelines for O&M services.

The guidelines maintain that for students to achieve their full potential, they must have access to an expanded core curriculum of instruction in skills related to their visual impairments, including

O&M. It is not appropriate to serve students who are visually impaired or blind solely through the general education curriculum or through a simplified curriculum because their disability-specific needs cannot be met through these channels. The least restrictive environment for such students may be an array of services, including O&M, not a physical location. A student's need for O&M may be one criterion that determines the most appropriate educational placement.

The population of students who are visually impaired or blind is diverse and includes those with additional disabilities. O&M must be a part of the assessment and programming processes and, according to these guidelines, should be conducted by certified O&M specialists. Students with low vision, who, because they may be independent in known environments, may not appear to need O&M services, should also be assessed and provided with services as appropriate. Infants and preschoolers who are visually impaired or blind, including those with additional disabilities, also require assessment and services from certified O&M specialists.

Appropriate assessment, planning, and instruction in O&M by certified O&M specialists is an exclusive right. No other service provider can assume this role. It is the responsibility of the state, region, and local district to furnish an adequate number of O&M specialists for their population of students who are visually impaired or blind. Similarly, the state and local agencies must promote O&M instruction that will extend beyond the physical limits of the school and hours of the typical school day. For example, some students' eye conditions produce visual limitations after dark so that they require instruction at night.

When fortified with pertinent legal knowledge, O&M specialists in the public schools are in firmer positions to act not only as teachers but as advocates for students who are visually impaired or blind. Doing so will help to ensure that students' unique needs are met in an appropriate and timely manner.

O&M Through
the School Year

The work of the O&M specialist in the public schools is tied to the cyclical schedules of the school year. By and large, the O&M specialist teaches when the students are present and has vacations when the students do. Different school districts may have different schedules. Some have school on a year-round basis, while others have traditional schedules. Still others have a combination of traditional and year-round schools. There are also extended or summer school programs. The work calendar of the O&M specialist is synchronized with the district's schedule or schedules according to his or her contract and the students' periods of attendance. The schedule may be assigned to the specialist or created with input and/or approval from the supervisor of the programs for students with visual impairments (see Setting Up a Schedule later in this chapter for further details). Some O&M specialists may work for a county or other education office and have to juggle the different calendars of several districts. Regardless of the type of schedule, each school year has a distinct beginning and end and semesters, quarters, and possibly trimesters, all of which are typically linked to the production of reports that evaluate students' progress.

In addition, all students receiving O&M services have an annual Individualized Education Program (IEP) meeting (or an Individualized Family Service Plan (IFSP) meeting for younger children) and additional IEP meetings as appropriate. An IEP is a written plan of instruction for students who receive special education services (see

Chapter 4 for further details). These meetings are scheduled on an individual basis and are not tied to preexisting school deadlines, such as those imposed by semesters or quarters.

THE BEGINNING OF THE SCHOOL YEAR

The beginning and end of each school year bring with them a number of necessary housekeeping tasks that promote and wrap up the usual activities of teaching that go on throughout the year. The long list of tasks at the beginning of the year include the following:

- finalizing a caseload
- reviewing records
- ascertaining enrollment
- making initial contact
- identifying yourself to school personnel
- scheduling assessments for new students
- scheduling observations
- setting up a schedule
- completing "off-campus" procedures
- obtaining a disabled parking permit
- evaluating canes
- issuing other materials
- gathering teaching materials
- obtaining workspace
- reviewing or creating an IEP calendar
- studying IEPs
- studying campuses and communities

These tasks are examined in the following sections.

Finalizing a Caseload

In the several days preceding the arrival of students at the beginning of the school year, the O&M specialist will be given, or participate in

establishing, a final roster of students representing his caseload or "class." A tentative or preliminary roster may have been set up at the end of the previous school year, in the interest of being prepared for the students upon their arrival after summer vacation.

Reviewing Records

Deciding when to review records is an individual choice. Some prefer to observe or meet a student before they read records because records can sometimes give a one-dimensional or misleading picture of a student. Others choose to read records before they see a student. The files of a single O&M student can contain a staggering amount of information, which may pose a significant challenge to those who do not have photographic memories, including such basic information as the following:

- the student's name and personal information
    birth date
    address
    phone number
    parents' or guardians' names

- the diagnosis gleaned from the eye care specialist's vision report

- the visual acuities and fields stated on the vision report

- the visual acuities and fields derived from the functional vision assessment (these frequently differ from those in the vision report; the functional vision assessment is discussed in more detail in Chapter 3)

- information concerning
    stereopsis
    contrast vision
    color vision
    the presence of light sensitivity

- information concerning aids or devices the student uses
- important miscellaneous information, including medically pertinent data

When an O&M specialist has a caseload of 12 to 15 students, sifting out significant information and making it immediately accessible and useful can be a challenge. The O&M Student Data Quick Reference Chart

O&M STUDENT DATA QUICK REFERENCE CHART

Student, Personal Information	Diagnosis	Clinical Visual Acuity, Functional Vision Assessment Acuity, Visual Fields	Stereopsis, Color Vision, Contrast, Photophobia	Aids or Devices	Miscellaneous
Audun, Thomas Date of birth 8/07 2nd grade (Parents) Tom & Alice 320 Kelsey, Woodland (Parents) 722-3890 (GP) 757-2187	Lebers Congenital amaurosis Light perception Light projection	Fields: Temporal 30° Inferior, superior 20°	No stereopsis No color Contrast: very slight	Cane Glasses Cane holder	Wears glasses to diminish eye poking.
Bynum, Tamara DoB 03/18 (Mother) Marie Grade 8 1500 Contra Costa Ridgemont 727-3180	Cerebral palsy Moderate-severe optic atrophy variable left eye turn R: moderate hyperopia astigmatism L: Mild myopia astigmatism	Visually Evoked Potential 20/512 - 20/353 Brief fixation	VEP indicates reduced contrast vision Severe restricted visual field suggested	Power chair	Present things directly in front of her. Takes Depakote Painful muscle contractures left hip
Trimble, LaTanya DoB 7/18 Grade10 (Mother) Anita 2020 Coronado Pocono Hills M. work (515) 602-1231, x 1320 Home: 731-9067	Retinopathy of prematurity Nystagmus Asthma	R: 20/200 L: Scleral shell Eye movement to R. more difficult than to L. Field: 80° from center to R. 30° from center to L. Amsler grid shows scotomas	No stereopsis	Glasses prescribed for protection only 6X monocular prescribed	Asthma Uses Albuterol If severe shortness of breath, call 911

Student	Eye Condition	Visual Acuity	Color / Light	Optical Devices	Medical / Other
Wong, Andrew DoB 11/22 Grade7 (Parents) Phil and Kathi 927 Mission, El Centro (Parents) 228-9111 (Father) cell 723-0029	Possible Lebers congenital amaurosis Progressive rod-cone dystrophy • irregular fixation • variable eccentric viewing, night blindness	Both eyes 20/160 in ambient Light. 20/2300 dim light Fields: light dependent-none in low light. ambient light: R. & inferior 60° superior 30°; L. 45°	Severe red green, yellow-blue defects Light sensitive Has photo gray glasses	Glasses Cane Visor 7 x 20 monocular- Also likes binoculars Cane holder	
Uribe, Angela DoB 11/22 Grade7 (Parents) Esverilda & Jorge 730 Mountain, Corona, (Parents) 504-2779 (Mother, work) 322-7850 (Father, work) 322-8001	Diabetes mellitus Optic nerve atrophy	Clinical, both eyes 20/125 Functional R. 20/240 L. 20/280 RLL Fields: 80° RLL	Some problems with depth perception Color deficiency, although names primary and secondary colors	Glasses won't help.	Takes insulin by injection 2Xs a day Checks sugar 5Xs a day Carries sugar at all times
Potts, Michael DoB 5/18 PreK (Parents) Tony & Don 1217 Durham #5, Ridgemont (Parents) 727-1799 (Father, work) 228-1921	Global developmental delays Cortical visual impairment Seizures Moderate spastic cerebral palsy	Clincial visual acuity: unable to measure at this time Functional visual acuity: negotiates large obstacles in classroom	Unable to measure at this time No light sensitivity apparent	Helmet	Must wear helmet at all times Phenobarbitol

FIGURE 2.1 **Form for Organizing Information about Students**

in Figure 2.1 is an example of a form in which the facts may be organized. It's a good idea to complete this form in pencil to accommodate changes.

Identifying Yourself to School Personnel

As an itinerant O&M specialist, you are not a regular staff member, but one of several visiting support personnel at each school you serve. It is essential to identify yourself to the principal, secretary, security guards, and other site personnel on your first contact with a school. Introducing yourself serves two purposes. First, it helps to establish the legitimacy of your presence. Second, later on in the term, it may help to forestall the interference of well-intentioned people bent on helping visually impaired students immersed in an O&M lesson who appear to be lost. When they see you in the vicinity, they will be less likely to rush to the aid of the student who is in the process of struggling toward independence. For a further discussion of issues related to identification, see the section, Keeping Safe as a Teacher in Chapter 9.

Verifying Enrollment

When the students first arrive in September, it is important to ascertain that the students in your caseload are actually enrolled and present, or at least expected, at their designated schools. Verify your student's enrollment with the school secretary at each school.

Making Initial Contact

Once you have located all your students, you can begin to introduce yourself to each student and his or her teacher or teachers and parents. Introductions to family members may need to be by telephone if they work outside the home during the day.

Scheduling Assessment for New Students

If there are new students who may require O&M services, initial assessments should be scheduled to determine their needs. (See Chapter 3 for detailed information about conducting assessments.)

Scheduling Observations

It may be advisable to do observations of unfamiliar students before you formally meet them. In this way, you can retain a measure of anonymity while observing and thus, it is hoped, see the student in a more natural light (see the section on Direct Observations in Chapter 3).

Setting Up a Schedule

To serve students on a regular basis, it is necessary to set up a regular service schedule. In the best of all possible worlds, scheduling draws heavily on the science of time management. However, in the realm of the public schools, different schools' schedules rarely coincide. Matters are further complicated by the observance of a crazy quilt of "minimum days" or half days, when school days are shortened for various reasons, in schools whose borders overlap those of schools that are not observing the same minimum days. The students' class and individual schedules and special activity days create additional scheduling conflicts.

Students are often scattered across miles of urban, suburban, and rural areas, with occasional clusters in special classes. Invariably they require different levels of service, ranging from frequent, direct service to occasional monitoring. To make matters even more complicated, it is important to schedule some lessons on the basis of a student's unique travel needs to teach skills within the context of the school day. For example, some students need to be scheduled so as to teach them to descend the stairs of the school bus and travel to their (often distant) classroom, making a stop at the bathroom on the way. Sidebar 2.1 presents some guidelines that can help O&M specialists who are responsible for establishing their own schedules make the most efficient use of their own and their students' time.

The schedule is a teacher's road map for daily activities. When used in conjunction with a calendar, it tells you where to be and when. When distributed and posted, it lets others know your whereabouts. A workable schedule includes the following information:

- names of students
- inclusive times of lessons
- school and site names
- predictable schedule variations, such as seeing a student every other week

When putting together a schedule, it is important to include, not only teaching time, but time for other necessary activities, such as these:

SIDEBAR 2.1 **Tips for Scheduling**

* Avoid scheduling the student during core subjects by reviewing the student's schedule and consulting with his or her guidance counselor.

* When a student is served several times a week, stagger the O&M schedule, so the student does not miss the same subject each time.

* For off-campus lessons, if it is permissible, schedule the student after school on regularly scheduled minimum days.

* When prolonged lessons in the community or on public transportation are necessary, schedule them after school hours, if permissible.

* For secondary students who require prolonged lessons, meet with the school guidance counselor prior to class scheduling and request that an elective, and possibly a physical education class, be scheduled back to back at the end of the school day so that the student can be scheduled for O&M lessons during these nonacademic subjects without having the time constraint of returning for more classes.

* When there are several students at the same site, schedule them back to back, when possible, to alleviate loss of time and excessive driving.

* Schedule regular consultation periods with teachers during lunch and before and after teaching hours so that the consultation periods are contiguous with the block of time that you serve the student or students at that site.

* Schedule the student in cooperation with the other specialists who work with him or her, such as the speech, occupational, and physical therapists.

* Schedule a block of flexible time to perform ongoing observations, to make home visits for preschoolers, to assess and process referrals, and to provide monitoring and consultation to students who may be served monthly or quarterly. When possible, it is advisable to schedule this time to accommodate students who are on half-day schedules, such as preschoolers and kindergartners.

* planning lessons and preparing materials

* monitoring performance and progress for students who do not receive direct O&M services, modeling teaching approaches for other staff members, and consulting with other staff and parents

* travel between sites

* lunch

* regular staff meetings

* processing referrals

- conducting observations and assessments
- writing reports
- making home visits

Figure 2.2 gives an example of a typical O&M teacher's schedule.

Once a viable schedule for serving students has been established, it is important to distribute copies to important others for legal and informational purposes. In particular, it is essential to give copies to the students' teachers and parents and the site administrators. If several students are concentrated in a single special class, it is advisable to post their schedules visibly so that substitute teachers and classroom aides will be informed.

It is also important to implement an *absence notification system* so that if the student is absent, you can reschedule your day in advance to use the time efficiently. It can be wasteful and frustrating to drive many miles to deliver an O&M lesson and find that the student is out with the flu. Any responsible person can be designated to communicate a student's absence. Mature students can be taught to report their absences themselves by calling the teacher's home, office, cellular telephone, or answering service and leaving a message if necessary. Parents, classroom teachers, or school secretaries may perform this function for younger students. In some situations, it may be impossible to set up a reliable absence notification system. It is then advisable to call the student's school or home in advance of the lesson to determine if he or she is present, particularly if there is a pattern of absenteeism.

Completing "Off-Campus" Procedures

When the schedule is established, it is necessary to complete paperwork to legalize taking students "off campus" into the community by car, walking, or public transportation, getting written permission from parents and administrators. Forms and procedures vary from district to district, but some samples are shown here. An O&M Instruction Permission form (Figure 2.3) is sent to parents annually to obtain permission to take a student off campus in accordance with the schedule. It is accompanied by the student's O&M schedule (Figure 2.4), which lists days, dates, times, destinations, and means of transportation for off-campus lessons. The O&M instructor may also send a map of the area where the lessons will take place, such as the school neighbor-

ORIENTATION AND MOBILITY SCHEDULE

TEACHER: Natalie Knott

DATE: September 27

	Monday	Tuesday	Wednesday	Thursday	Friday	Schools and Students
8:00	Ocean View Preparation period	Office Preparation period	Ocean View Preparation period	Office Preparation period	Miscellaneous Sites * Conferences * Staff, parent training * Observation and assessment of referrals. * Home visits * Report writing	Anderson High LaTanya Trimble Edward Lee Antonio LaSelva Thomas Antonelli Bob Hanson Cecelia Young
8:30	Annie Ortega campus		Annie Ortega 1st, 3rd, 5th weeks—school neighborhood 2nd, 4th—home neighborhood			M.L. King Middle School Pat Han Tamara Bynum Thomas Czechi
9:00		Transit		Transit		Chavez Elementary Brent Tucker Erin Long
9:30	Transit	Chavez Elementary Brent Tucker 1st, 3rd, 5th weeks—school neighborhood 2nd, 4th—Safeway	Transit	Anderson High Antonio LaSelva Greater community public transportation lessons		Ocean View Annie Ortega
10:00	M.L. King Middle School Tamara Bynum		M.L. King Middle School Thomas Czechi 1st, 3rd, 5th weeks—school neighborhood 2nd, 4th—Safeway			Springfield Candace Zackman Karen Markham
10:30	1st, 3rd, 5th weeks—school neighborhood 2nd, 4th—Safeway	Erin Long 1st, 3rd, 5th weeks—home neighborhood				Vista Colina David Winters
11:00	Pat Han, 1st, 3rd, 5th—home neighborhood 2nd, 4th—Safeway	2nd, 4th, Safeway	Transit	Lunch	Transit	
11:30			Anderson High Lunch Conference Mrs. Wang *Every other week* Office VI and O&M department meeting	*Every other week* Instructional assistants conferences, trainings	M.L. King Middle School Pat Han—campus	
12:00	Transit	Lunch Transit			Transit	

12:30	<u>Anderson High</u> Lunch	<u>Springfield</u> Candace Lackman— campus		<u>Lunch</u>	
1:00	Thomas Antonelli 1st, 3rd, 5th weeks— campus 2nd, 4th, school neighborhood	Karen Markham— campus	Preparation period	Thomas Antonelli 1st, 3rd, 5th weeks— school neighborhood 2nd, 4th, Albertson's	<u>Anderson High</u> Cecilia Young
1:30		Teacher Conference Transit	Transit		
2:00	Preparation period	<u>Anderson High</u> Edward Lee 1st, 3rd, 5th weeks— campus 2nd, 4th—home neighborhood	<u>Vista Colina</u> David Winters 1st, 3rd, 5th weeks— home neighborhood 2nd—Albertson's 4th—Marina Vista Mall	Preparation period	Preparation period
2:30	LaTanya Trimble—Old Town			LaTanya Trimble 1st, 3rd, 5th weeks— Plaza del Norte 2nd, 4th—Marina Vista Mall	Edward Lee 1st, 3rd, 5th weeks— school neighborhood 2nd—Marina Vista Mall 4th—Plaza del Norte
3:00					
3:30					

(Diagonal note in the upper right cell: Every other week monitor — Bob Hanson)

FIGURE 2.2 **Sample Schedule for an O&M Teacher**

PROGRAM FOR VISUALLY IMPAIRED STUDENTS
ORIENTATION AND MOBILITY INSTRUCTION
PERMISSION STATEMENT

_____ *LaTanya Trimble* _____ has permission to participate

(Student's name)

in the Orientation and Mobility Program in the _____ *Oceanside School District* _____

(School District Name)

for the current school year. I understand that my child will be going off campus on a regular basis to learn safe and efficient travel skills. I also understand that my child always will be individually supervised by a teacher or student teacher under a teacher's supervision. The attached calendar lists dates, times, locations, and/or destinations and methods of transportation for specific lessons. I understand that lessons are sequential and proceed according to the rate of a student's progress. If the student is absent on lesson dates or proceeds more rapidly or slowly than anticipated, I will be notified of changes in the calendar activities.

I know that I must return this permission statement to my child's O&M teacher and that I may call him/her if I have questions about any of the activities.

Natalie Knott

O&M Specialist

222-1822

Telephone Number

Anita Trimble

Parent/Guardian Signature

September 10, 2002

Date

FIGURE 2.3 **Sample O&M Permission Form for Off-Campus Instruction**

STUDENT ORIENTATION AND MOBILITY SCHEDULE

YEAR ___2002–03___

STUDENT ___LaTanya Trimble___

O&M SPECIALIST ___Natalie Knott___

This schedule (and map) will cover the period of ___September 15–January 1___

If changes in plans are to be made, you will be sent an update or new schedule to approve.

Thank you,

___Natalie Knott___
O&M Specialist

P.S. If you have any questions or concerns, please phone me at ___222-1822___

P.P.S. On days when the weather is very stormy, lessons will be conducted at school.

DAY/DATES	TIME	DESTINATION	TRANSPORTATION
MONDAYS—all	between 2:30 and 3:30	Old Town: along Canal Boulevard between 2nd and 22nd Streets	Teacher's car and walking
THURSDAYS 1st, 3rd, 5th	between 2:30 and 3:30	Del Norte Plaza	Teacher's car and walking
2nd, 4th	between 2:30 and 3:30	Marina Vista Mall	Teacher's car

FIGURE 2.4 **Sample Student O&M Lesson Schedule**

hood. The schedule may be updated periodically as the student progresses. An O&M update form (Figure 2.5) can be used to obtain the parents' permission to change the student's regular schedule.

Obtaining a Disabled Parking Permit

When an O&M specialist transports students who are legally blind or have low vision and other qualifying disabilities, it is a good idea to obtain a special parking permit that allows him or her to park in the parking places reserved for people with disabilities in the community. These permits are usually issued by the Department of Motor Vehicles. They save time, promote safety in parking lots, and provide opportunities to teach the students about some of their rights as people with disabilities.

Evaluating Canes and Other Materials

The beginning of the school year is an excellent time to evaluate the condition of cane users' canes to see if they need to be repaired and whether the length is still appropriate. A student may grow several inches over the summer and need a longer cane, or a cane may have become damaged. When a new cane is needed, it may be ordered from a vendor (see the Resources section) or loaned to the student from a cane library maintained by the school district's program for visually impaired students, or the student may be supported in helping to order the cane (for further information and sample forms, see the section on Cane Travel in Chapter 7). The beginning of the year is also a time to issue or reissue other special devices or materials, such as cane holders, visors, or telescopes, which will help the students to function more effectively and independently.

Gathering Teaching Materials

Prior to teaching, it is necessary to assemble a variety of teaching and related materials and to store them either in the car trunk, for ready access from a number of sites, or at the sites where you work with the students. (For details on what these materials consist of, see the section, The Well-Equipped Teacher in Chapter 9.)

Obtaining Workspace

At times, O&M specialists require access to specific workspaces to conduct assessments and work on motor, conceptual, or O&M-related

PROGRAM FOR VISUALLY IMPAIRED STUDENTS
ORIENTATION AND MOBILITY UPDATE

LaTanya Trimble _____ has my permission to participate in
_____Student Name_____

Orientation and Mobility instruction to:

_____ _Marina Vista Mall_ _____ by _____ _city bus #18_ _____
_____Destination_____   _____Mode of transportation_____

on _____ _Tuesdays 11/6, 13, 20, 27_ _____ between _____ _11:50 a.m. and 2:10 p.m.._ _____
_____Date(s)_____   _____(time)_____

I understand that this update indicates a change in plans for _____ _the month of November_ _____
_____Time Period_____

_____ _Natalie Knott_ _____
O&M Instructor

_____ _222-1822_ _____
Telephone Number

Anita Trimble _____
Parent/Guardian Signature

October 25, 2002 _____
Date

FIGURE 2.5 **Sample Form for Updating Student's O&M Schedule**

living skills (such as telephone skills). Space is not automatically assigned, so it needs to be requested from the site supervisor or school secretary. Whether the space is to be used on a regular or onetime basis, it is often necessary to reserve it in advance.

With the teacher's permission, it may be possible to set up shop in a corner of a resource room or special class for students with visual impairments, provided that the activities of the student and other students are not mutually distracting. Related details can be worked out with the classroom teacher. Some facilities have a motor room where occupational and physical therapists work with students to develop or increase their gross or fine motor skills using equipment such as swings, trampolines, bicycles, stairs, slides, and ball pools. This is also an excellent O&M environment if you can get access to use it. The nurse's office can become a lab for working on telephone skills. In the event that no such spaces are available, it is necessary to be more flexible and resourceful. For example, the auditorium stage is an excellent area to work on motor skills, and though not the first choice, hallways and storage rooms can be adapted in a pinch.

It is advisable in some instances to secure storage space for learning materials and equipment, especially when working with preschool and elementary-aged students who are grouped in special classes. Some objects, such as tricycles and sound systems, are too bulky or cumbersome to carry from the car to a site and back to the car. When large quantities of materials are used regularly at a single site, it is a good idea to have specially assigned storage space. The space should be conveniently located, readily accessible to you at all times, and secure from theft or misappropriation.

Reviewing or Creating an IEP Calendar and Studying IEPs

Each student with an established IEP has an annual calendar date by which time it is necessary to have conducted an IEP meeting to update concerns, progress, and/or goals and objectives for instruction. Keeping on top of IEPs can be no mean feat, especially with regard to completing assessments in time to write the annual reports and IEPs before the scheduled meetings. It helps to keep an IEP calendar that lists students and their projected IEP meeting dates in chronological order with reference to their previous year's dates (see Figure 2.6 for an example). This calendar gives an annual overview of approximate due dates, which makes planning much easier and relieves some of the pressure associated with meeting deadlines. An overview keeps IEP dates from sneaking up with the turn of a calendar's page or the arrival of an unexpected summons to an IEP meeting for a student. Projected dates based on last year's due dates may be penciled in and then replaced by actual dates when they are confirmed. This will allow you to plan accordingly and give you enough time to assess students and write their respective reports and IEPs in compliance with the individual deadlines. Examining students' current IEPs helps to establish an appropriate focus and allows you to create lesson plans for the initial lesson or lessons.

Studying Campuses and Communities

It is important to become familiar with the layouts of the students' schools and to obtain maps of the schools, when necessary. Similarly, studying the neighboring communities helps one to start planning strategies for off-campus lessons.

THE REST OF THE SCHOOL YEAR

During the majority of the school year, O&M specialists are occupied with all activities related to ongoing instruction of the students in their caseloads as well as ongoing monitoring of other students and consultations with staff members and parents. In addition, new students are being referred for O&M services throughout the year, so observations and assessments for them may need to be scheduled at any time. There are also ongoing assessments of students' performance and a variety of reports that need to be completed throughout the year.

The Individuals with Disabilities Education Act (IDEA) mandates that students receiving special education services get progress reports or report cards like their peers in general education. These reports are linked to the goals and objectives of each student's IEP (see Chapter 4) and are usually issued at the time of general education report cards (which students who are in general education classes will also receive). Therefore, it is necessary to assess each student's progress in the several designated areas and write and distribute two to four report cards per student each year.

ANNUAL IEP CALENDAR

Date	Time	Place	Student's name	Completed
September 27	2:10	Room 5	LaTanya Trimble	✓
October 15	2:45	Room 10	Thomas Antonelli	✓
October 22	3:15	M 306	Tamara Bynum	✓
October 31	8:00 a.m.	Conference room	Andrew Wong	✓
November 12	4:10	H505	Pat Han	✓
December 17	3:45	Room 15	Susan Weeks	
February 7			Cecilia Young	
March 18			Michael Potts	
March 21			Burt Tucker	
April 11			Angela Uribe	
May 2			Candy Folkman	
June 11			Karen Markham	
June 13			Antonio LaSelva	

FIGURE 2.6 **Sample IEP Calendar for an O&M Instructor**

As was noted earlier, each student also needs to be evaluated for his or her new IEP at the designated time in the school year. A meeting or meetings will be held, and the revised IEP must be written.

THE END OF THE SCHOOL YEAR

There are several housekeeping activities at the end of the school year that help to tie up loose ends and prepare for the summer and the year ahead. This is a good time to check the condition of canes, do necessary repairs and cleaning, and size and reissue canes for the summer, as needed. Items that have been temporarily loaned to students are checked back in. The cane inventory can be reviewed and orders prepared for the next year.

This chapter has given a brief overview of a typical school year for an O&M specialist working in a public school system. If you have gone through the long list of tasks covered in this chapter, you will be well prepared for the school year and ready to begin teaching. The next two chapters focus in more detail on some of the crucial tasks that lay the basis for direct instruction: assessing newly referred students and participating in writing students' IEPs.

Referral and Assessment

When students who are blind or visually impaired are first evaluated to determine whether orientation and mobility (O&M) services may be appropriate, they are referred to the O&M specialist for assessment to ascertain their experiences, knowledge, abilities, and areas of need. Such referrals may be made at any time during the school year. Students who are not currently receiving O&M services come to the attention of the O&M specialist by several means.

Some students are referred for assessment when they are initially considered candidates for the services of the program for visually impaired students in the school district. Still others are referred from within the program as they develop a need for O&M services. It is not uncommon for a student to receive O&M services intermittently at different levels in his or her school career as new age-appropriate needs arise. For example, once an elementary student becomes a competent traveler at home, in school, and in the home and school communities, he or she may be discontinued until a further need arises, such as the transition to the next level of schooling when a change in site presents new challenges.

A variety of people may refer a student for O&M services—virtually anyone who observes the need. In most instances, the referral is made by a teacher who is closely involved with the student, such as a special day-class teacher of students with visual impairments or an itinerant teacher of students with visual impairments. Parents also refer their children. At times, a referral is made by an eye care special-ist or an administrator. Occasionally students refer themselves.

Other students enter the school district from another district with current Individualized Education Programs (IEPs) that include O&M services. In such cases, the O&M specialist may choose to continue with the present levels of service indicated and follow through on the current goals and objectives. However, it is advisable to assess trans-ferring students to:

- determine whether the levels of service are appropriate
- determine whether goals and objectives are current and appro-priate, especially in the new setting
- pinpoint areas of strength and need
- increase knowledge of a student's personality and performance

THE REFERRAL PROCESS

The specific procedures for referring a student for O&M services vary according to the official policies and procedures of the school district in question. In the interest of simplicity, this chapter considers the process from the point at which the O&M specialist receives the referral.

Once the student has come to the specialist's attention through official channels, the specialist needs to prepare for assessment by com-pleting all pertinent paperwork and obtaining the authorization from the parents or guardians required by the school district for observa-tions and assessments, including the following steps:

- Record significant information about the student.
- Start taking anecdotal records.
- Obtain the vision report.
- Obtain a hearing evaluation report.
- For students with functional vision, obtain a functional vision assessment.
- Complete procedures, including any legal releases necessary, for conducting an O&M assessment.

The O&M specialist needs to record all pertinent and available information about each student. The Orientation and Mobility Referral form (see Figure 3.1) is an example of a form that organizes important information about a student. This form may be used as is or adapted to fit specific needs. The person who refers the student for assessment may be asked to fill out such a form, particularly if that person is a teacher of students with visual impairments, because the teacher may already have the necessary information at his or her disposal. The form organizes the following data for each student who is referred for O&M services:

- student data or personal information

- medical data of vital concern

- vision data from vision reports

- hearing data from audiological reports

- information about low vision devices, such as eyeglasses, telescopes, visors, and sun shields

- background data concerning previous O&M training or perceived needs in this area

This is also the time to start keeping anecdotal records for the student. Anecdotal records are brief notes, in which all activities concerning a particular student, from the time of initial referral to the end of O&M services, are recorded. The dates of described activities, along with the time involved, are noted, as are brief descriptions of the types of contact and any noteworthy comments regarding issues related to assessment, progress, particular challenges, change in status, and so forth. At this point, for example, you may be noting your initial conversations with the student and the family. These notes can be made on a simple form that lists the student's name and the date and time of the activity and has room for comments. (For an example and additional discussion of anecdotal records, see Chapter 9.) These records are useful to refer back to in lesson planning, isolating problem areas, problem solving, establishing goals, and monitoring progress.

The O&M specialist needs to be sure to obtain a copy of each student's current vision report—the report of a clinical examination by an eye care professional, either an ophthalmologist or optometrist. This report may be immediately available in the student's file if the student is currently in the program for visually impaired students. If it is unavailable, it may be requested, with a parental release form, from the

ORIENTATION AND MOBILITY REFERRAL
BASIC INFORMATION

Student Data

Student Name _____ Date of Birth _____

Address _____ Telephone No. _____

Parent/Guardian Name _____ Telephone No. _____

Address _____ Work Telephone _____

Language Spoken at Home _____

School or Placement _____ Grade _____ Teacher _____ Room _____

Teacher of Students with Visual Impairments _____

Medical Data

Medical Conditions _____

_____

Medications Being Taken _____

_____

Special Procedures, Considerations _____

_____

Vision Data

Cause of Visual Impairment/Blindness:

O.D. _____

O.S. _____

Visual Acuity:

	Without Correction	With Correction	Field
	O.D. _____	O.D. _____	O.D. _____
	O.S. _____	O.S. _____	O.S. _____
	O.U. _____	O.U. _____	O.U. _____

Eye Care Specialist _____ Telephone _____

Address _____

Date of Most Recent Exam _____ Date Report Requested _____

FIGURE 3.1 **Sample O&M Referral Form**

Low Vision Clinic _____ Telephone _____

Address _____

Date of Most Recent Exam _____ Date Report Requested _____

Hearing Data

Cause of Hearing Loss _____

Hearing Loss (decibels)

        Right Ear: Aided _____   Unaided _____

        Left Ear: Aided _____   Unaided _____

Hearing Specialist _____ Telephone _____

Address _____

Date of Most Recent Exam _____ Date Report Requested _____

Low Vision Devices

Devices Prescribed/Recommended _____

_____

Devices Used (Include strength of optical devices, if known) _____

_____

Background Data

Source of Referral _____

Comments _____

_____

Previous O&M Training:

Agency, District, or Individual _____

Address _____ Telephone _____

Skill Level Attained _____

_____

Observed Needs, Type of Training Desired

_____

_____

student's eye care specialist. If the student has not been seen recently, or at all, by an eye care specialist, it is necessary to recommend that the parent or primary care giver arrange for a vision exam. It is also a good idea, if an appointment is to be made, to request information on the student's visual field and color vision, since this is essential information for the O&M specialist. In addition, if there is no evidence of a recent hearing evaluation, request that one be performed and obtain the records.

If the student has functional vision, the O&M specialist needs to determine whether the student has had a functional vision assessment and request a copy of the report. A functional vision assessment—as distinct from a clinical vision assessment—is an evaluation of a student's actual visual functioning under different conditions, in a variety of locations, while performing practical, real-life tasks. The report of such an assessment can give you valuable information about the student's vision and use of vision. It is particularly imperative to obtain information on a student's visual fields to determine whether there are field defects, since knowledge of visual field abnormalities is essential in assessing, training, and supervising a student in safe travel.

If there is no current functional vision assessment, it will be necessary for the O&M specialist or teacher of students with visual impairments to conduct one, or they may collaborate in conducting the assessment. (The details of this procedure are beyond the scope of this book; for discussions and guidelines regarding the process of functional vision assessment, see Anthony, 2000; Erin & Paul, 1996; Koenig et al., 2000.)

Finally, before a formal assessment can be conducted, it is necessary to fill out supporting documents to make it legal to take the student off campus and transport him or her by car or on public transportation for the assessment and subsequent lessons if the assessment reveals that O&M services are indicated. Procedures vary from district to district, each one having its own channels for handling off-campus procedures and gaining parents' permission. Figure 3.2 is an example of a form for obtaining permission to take a student out of school to conduct an O&M assessment. Other sample forms, shown in Chapter 2, can be used to obtain permission to participate in regular O&M instruction.

The completion of the preceding steps will provide both an informational and a legal foundation for conducting an O&M assessment. It

ORIENTATION AND MOBILITY ASSESSMENT
PERMISSION STATEMENT

I (would , would not) like my child, _____ to receive
   (cross out one)

an orientation and mobility assessment by _____
                                          (teacher name and phone number)

to determine whether he/she would benefit from instruction in travel skills that will enable him/her

to travel more efficiently and safely. This may include making supervised street crossings in residential

and business areas where there are stop signs and stoplights.

    I give permission to _____ to take my child

out of class and off campus for the assessment.

The date/time(s) for the assessment will be: _____

The location/destination will be: _____

The method of transportation to the assessment site will be:

_____ walking

_____ teacher's car

_____ public transportation

I know that I must return this permission statement to my child's teacher and that I may call him/her

if I have questions about this assessment.

_____

Parent/Guardian Signature

_____

Date

FIGURE 3.2 **Sample Permission Form for an O&M Assessment**

is also advisable to review other available information on the student, especially if the student has additional impairments or a history of being in special education programs.

CONDUCTING AN O&M ASSESSMENT

An O&M student's instructional program needs to be tailored specifically to that student's abilities and needs, as determined through the O&M specialist's assessment. An O&M assessment is based on information gathered from a variety of sources, including the students' records, additional informal observations and information gathering, and formal assessment of O&M skills.

Preliminary Information Gathering

Before conducting a formal assessment of a student's O&M skills, the O&M specialist will want to gather some general background information in addition to that found in the student's records. He or she can do so through direct observation of the student as well as interviews with family members, teachers, and the student.

Direct Observations

During direct observation, the O&M instructor spends a period of time focused purely on observing the student's abilities, including the following:

- motor skills
- use of assistive devices, such as a cane or a telescope
- safety and confidence
- sensory skills
- spatial orientation
- ability to follow directions

Observations of students may be recorded on a form, such as the Student Observation Form shown in Figure 3.3. This form may be used for observation during the initial assessment, as well as for routine observations of students who are currently receiving O&M services. There is a column to note the time periodically and a column to describe how the student performs different activities that have signif-

STUDENT OBSERVATION FORM

Student: _____Michael_____   Observer: _____Knott_____

Setting: __Initial Observation: Transition from Classroom__   Date: __September 7__

Time	Observations	Comments
11:50	Michael (M) gets up from last seat in row, makes 180° turn, shuffles 3 feet to cubbies arms outstretched. Finds cubby, backpack. Argues with instructional assistant (IA) about taking his cane.	(IA presents cane to him.) * Let student put backpack on first and get cane independently from wall cane holder. * Work w/ IA on appropriate independence, reinforcement of use of cane skills.
	M dons backpack, takes cane from IA and shuffles toward door with cane held up and forward, incorrect grip. Bumps into student at the end of the line. Stops, stands in line at door. M keeps standing (left behind).	(Line starts to move outside, classroom teacher looks back and tells student to go get M.) * Assign line partner to initiate contact and guide position before line starts to move.
	M takes student's wrist, then hand and follows for several feet with cane held up in front. M starts to run and pulls ahead of boy, pulling him along and then letting go, continuing at end of line but wide to the left.	In peril for collisions! * Teach shoulder guiding as alternative to human guiding. * Work on line skills in a context without pressures of a short lunch period and rapidly moving line.
11:55	IA leads him back to the boy and helps them assume human guide position. Position correct for a few steps, then M walks beside and wide of his guide.	* Plan lessons for route to the cafeteria. * Reinforce human guide wrist grasp position with IA and M.
	M still wide approaching door to breezeway. IA stops him from bumping into door frame, pushing him closer to the guide.	
	M drops his cane.	
	IA picks it up and takes M by the hand.	

FIGURE 3.3 Sample Student Observation Form

icance relative to his or her use of vision and O&M skills. A column for comments provides space for "editorial" remarks, memos, and pertinent quotes from other people regarding the student. In the example in Figure 3.3, the O&M specialist uses the comments column to note skills that need to be reinforced, ideas for modifying procedures, and plans for future lessons.

Some behaviors are best observed outside a testing situation. It is important to scrutinize a student's functional travel skills in several settings. The student should be observed in the *familiar* settings of home, classroom, school, and school yard. The student should also be observed in a setting that is totally *unfamiliar* to him or her. It is important to include an unfamiliar setting because students often appear to be competent and confident travelers in familiar environments, but may undergo a transformation in unfamiliar settings, exhibiting reduced confidence, altered gait and posture, poor orientation, and characteristics of absent depth perception and poor contrast vision. When conducted to an unfamiliar place, a student who walks freely around school may shuffle and grope or go down on his or her hands and knees to test or negotiate ground-level obstacles, shadows, and uneven terrain. An unfamiliar urban park can provide an excellent observation site when it contains distant landmarks; uneven terrain; varied ground textures, such as gravel, grass, sand, and wood mulch; and a variety of ground-level obstacles, stairs, and climbing equipment.

Interviews with Parents, Teachers, and the Student

Some formal O&M assessments (see the next section on selecting assessment instruments) contain interview components, relying to some degree on reports from parents or other individuals who are familiar with the student. O&M specialists can develop their own interview questions or use published interview formats, such as those included in the TAPS curriculum (Pogrund et al., 1995). In either case, it is always a good idea to have a list of questions prepared ahead of time to avoid forgetting something.

Interviews can yield a wealth of useful information, including the following:

- perceived needs and abilities of the student

- areas of concern

- possible performance goals

- diagnostic information

- medications taken, including side effects

- previous O&M instruction

- use of assistive devices

Interviews with parents and teachers may be informal and may be part of the process of introducing yourself to them. They can also be useful to fill in information that is missing from the student's records or previous assessments. During such interviews, it is possible to identify concerns and goals reflecting the student's needs in the three basic domains of home, school, and community.

Selecting Assessment Instruments

Ideally an O&M assessment is a complex and multifaceted procedure that addresses the unique abilities and needs of the student. The realm of O&M assessment encompasses the following areas:

- attending behaviors

- receptive language for commands

- body image

- concepts of direction, position, and quantity

- color identification

- geometric shapes

- textures and contours

- basic skills

- cane techniques

- O&M in the home

- O&M at school

- personal information

- map skills

- cardinal directions

- use of optical aids

- residential-area travel and street crossings

- address systems

- business-area travel

- light-controlled intersections and crossings

- public transportation

- shopping/consumer skills

- social skills

A formal O&M assessment generally involves selected activities in predetermined environments. After the preliminary information-gathering procedures have been performed, the O&M specialist will have information regarding the student's abilities, skills, needs, level of independence, and use of assistive devices. This information will help the O&M specialist select the appropriate areas for formal assessment. A number of well-designed assessment instruments are available, both published and unpublished, that serve various types and ages of students and measure different aspects and levels of skills and development (see the Resources section for a list of some formal O&M assessments). The O&M specialist will develop a repertoire of assessment instruments to choose from, depending on the individual students' needs. It may be necessary to use a combination of assessments to yield an accurate profile of present, absent, and emerging skills. The O&M specialist will need to match assessments and/or sections of assessments to the student with regard to age, experience, cognitive level, behavioral issues (when present), and range of additional disabilities.

Sidebar 3.1 offers additional tips for conducting assessments. (For additional details about O&M assessment, see Fazzi & Petersmeyer, 2001.) A summary of all the information collected during a student's assessment will be the foundation on which to build the student's educational goals and eventual lesson plans.

Evaluation Routes

Evaluation routes are used to determine current levels of skills for students for whom the learning of community travel skills is appropriate. Age, ability, cognitive level, previous experience, and travel needs are taken into consideration when deciding whether a student should be assessed using evaluation routes.

SIDEBAR 3.1 **Tips for Assessment**

---

* An assessment may take several hours. It may be desirable to separate it into different periods on different days to prevent the student from becoming fatigued.

* Prior to assessing, it is important to ascertain whether the student is well, is adequately rested, and has eaten breakfast. If testing is scheduled just before lunch, optimum results may not be achieved because the student is hungry.

* When an assessment is to be conducted out of doors, it is important to determine if the student is properly clothed for the weather. Sometimes students arrive at school over- or underdressed. For example, a student without warm clothes on a winter day will be distracted by the cold and may not perform well.

* Check to see if the student has the necessary assistive devices (eyeglasses, telescope, cane, and so forth). Conducting an assessment on a student whose eyeglasses are broken or lost will give misleading results.

* If an assessment environment is to be prepared indoors at the school, to make best use of the student's time,

  1. make sure the location is obtained in advance; it may be necessary to sign up in the school office for a room.

  2. make sure the location is distraction-free.

  3. prepare the environment before the assessment, for example, by adjusting lighting and seating for the student's comfort.

  4. have all assessment materials on hand, organized, and ready to present, including assessment forms, pencil or pen, assessment kits, necessary manipulatives, and any other items related to specific skills being assessed, such as a map, a compass, pictures of body parts, Chang Kit, Wheatley Tactile Diagram Kit, and so forth.

* When using a preexisting environment for an assessment, for example, a location in the community, be sure it presents opportunities to assess all skills required. For example, when assessing street-crossing skills, are intersections appropriately varied? Will adequate traffic be present at the time of the assessment?

It is helpful to have fixed evaluation routes encompassing areas that provide opportunities to measure all skills essential to safe and efficient travel. Having these routes ensures thoroughness and consistency. However, it may not be possible if students are spread across a wide geographic area. In such cases, a variety of sites can be used to conduct the evaluations.

Low Vision

Low vision evaluations are conducted with students who have low vision to measure functional vision *and* O&M skills simultaneously. There are several factors that affect the outcome of a low vision evaluation. Students may perform differently according to the weather and the resulting illumination. A bright sunny day produces contrast and glare, whereas an overcast day reduces contrast. The time of day is similarly significant. When the sun is overhead, there is less glare and back lighting than in the morning and afternoon. Traffic density also varies according to the time of day and from day to day. Rush-hour traffic creates greater challenges to a neophyte traveler than does midmorning traffic. Periods of traffic lull may fail to produce adequate sound cues or conditions to measure a student's ability to make safe choices. All these factors should be weighed when choosing an evaluation period and interpreting the evaluation of a particular student. The student's unique visual condition must also be figured into the equation. Ideally, a low vision evaluation route would include the following:

- residential crossings at uncontrolled and sign-controlled intersections.
- business-district crossings at busy uncontrolled and light-controlled intersections (including pedestrian lights)
- the location of specific objectives, such as stores, departments, and items, and a bus stop
- returning to the point of origin by an alternate route

Throughout the evaluation, functional vision is being assessed along with travel skills. When the evaluation is concluded, the O&M specialist should have a picture of the student's near, distance, and color vision and his or her ability to target objects and see details and motion. Also measured are the student's ability to cross at sign- and light-controlled intersections, to familiarize himself or herself with a store, to use efficient search patterns, and to follow directions and retain orientation. Similarly, the student's posture and gait, object negotiation, line projection (ability to travel in a straight line without veering), and response to lighting can be assessed.

Business Area

A business-area evaluation presupposes advanced street-crossing skills and measures travel skills required to access and use business areas. Ideally, the route would give opportunities for assessing the following skills:

- locating a bus stop
- identifying the appropriate bus
- riding a bus to a designated stop
- traveling within a shopping mall and locating specific objectives
- traveling within a department store, locating objectives, making a purchase, and using the escalator and elevator
- reversing the route and returning to the point of origin

Rapid Transit

A rapid-transit evaluation measures a student's skills in using a rapid transit system. The evaluation presupposes the ability to use a bus, but when advisable, the bus segment could be omitted. Ideally, the route would present opportunities for measuring the following skills:

- locating a rapid transit station
- performing negotiations within the station, such as buying a fare card or token and using it appropriately in a turnstile, adding fare to a fare card when necessary, and finding and using public assistance when necessary
- traveling within the station
- locating the appropriate boarding point
- identifying the appropriate train
- riding the train to a designated stop in a neighboring city
- exiting the station
- locating objectives within the neighboring city
- reversing the route and returning to the point of origin

PUTTING IT ALL TOGETHER

When the referral, information-gathering, and assessment procedures are completed, the O&M specialist will be able to construct a comprehensive picture of a student's current strengths and weaknesses. The

O&M specialist generally compiles the combined information into a formal report. The format of this report will differ depending on the school district, the individual instructor, and the amount of detail needed to appropriately represent the student, but the assessment report for Angela shown in Figure 3.4 is a good example. This assessment will form the basis for writing the O&M portion of the student's annual IEP, which includes the student's present levels of O&M skills and short- and long-term instructional goals. Chapter 4 discusses in detail the process of developing a student's IEP.

Ongoing assessments throughout the year will measure the student's progress and determine when new goals and objectives should be set. Assessment is not confined to the period of initial contact with an incoming student, but is an integral part of providing a relevant, individualized, ongoing O&M program that grows and changes with the student. Periodic assessment will continue throughout the student's career in O&M.

Oceana Unified School District

ORIENTATION AND MOBILITY ASSESSMENT REPORT

Name: Angela Uribe

DOB: 07/22/90

School: M. L. King Middle School

Assessor: Natalie Knott, Teacher of Students with Visual Impairment & O&M Specialist

Reason: Student has a visual impairment

Evaluation Date: 11/30/02

Background Information

Angela is a 12-year-old seventh-grade student who is in the Visually Impaired Program and receives support in a resource room for students with visual impairment. She uses large print and a closed-circuit television to enlarge materials that have not been enlarged, such as tests. She reports that she uses glasses for doing homework, but that it is difficult to adjust to them and that she has "tried out" a monocular telescope, but that it was difficult to locate objects with it.

Etiology

Angela was diagnosed with insulin-dependent diabetes at age 3 years. An eye report, dated 4/20, states Angela has the syndrome of diabetes and optic atrophy, with a measured visual acuity of 20/125. A functional vision assessment conducted in December 2000 reports the following:

- Her right eye appears to be stronger.
- There appears to be some difficulty in depth assessment.
- She appears to have a color vision deficiency.
- Her functional vision as measured in a class room setting is 20/200 with both eyes for near.

Means of Assessment

Angela was assessed through the following means:

- Review of records.
- Interview with student, parents.
- Orientation & Mobility Low Vision Evaluation.
- TAPS (Teaching Age Appropriate Purposeful Skills) Assessment.
- Teacher observation.

FIGURE 3.4 **Sample O&M Assessment Report**

Body Image

Angela's body image is well developed and age appropriate. She demonstrates knowledge of simple and complex body parts, body movements, body planes, and objects in relationship to herself.

Laterality

Angela demonstrates appropriate knowledge of laterality (left and right awareness) for functional use in orientation and mobility (O&M).

Quantitative Concepts

She demonstrates functional knowledge of comparative sizes.

Directional and Positional Concepts

She demonstrates functional use of positional and directional concepts, with the exception of "perpendicular."

Color

Angela names primary and secondary colors at near and at a distance.

Geometric Shapes

Angela identifies a variety of geometric shapes including the octagon.

Cardinal Directions

Angela can identify the opposite directions of North/South and East/West. She has not used a compass and had some difficulty identifying East and West in relation to herself when facing a wall that was verbally identified as North and when asked to make corresponding turns to face East and West from her original position of facing North.

Personal Information

Angela tells her address with prompts to say her city and zip code. She states her phone number with a prompt for area code. She states her height and weight.

On-Campus Orientation and Mobility

Angela is oriented to her campus and classrooms and travels independently and confidently at school.

Residential Area Travel

Angela identifies some components of a residential area such as *sidewalk, curb, crosswalk,* and *gutter*. She has difficulty reading signs in the environment at a distance and was unable to locate or read a 4-inch house address on a door from 6 feet. She described a black-and-white one-way sign across a two-lane street and identified the arrow.

FIGURE 3.4 **Sample O&M Assessment Report** (continued)

At the first street, when asked to position herself for a crossing, she stood 2 feet back from the curb so that a telephone pole blocked her view of oncoming traffic in the far lane. When prompted to step close to the curb and asked to determine when a safe time to cross would be, she scanned in all directions including left and behind. She then identified when it was safe and crossed with the assessor's supervision. She did not scan during the crossing. At the second crossing, her scan was less thorough and she made a false start when a car was approaching.

Business Area Travel

Angela could not locate a white fire hydrant on the corner ahead of her and eventually passed it. When asked to turn back so that it was about 3 feet away and to look left she did not notice it until the assessor pointed to it. She may have expected it to be red.

At a light-controlled intersection, she positioned herself to cross to the left of the crosswalk lines and required several prompts to identify the crosswalk lines and to move to an appropriate position between them on the curb. She could not locate or identify traffic lights and changes across four lanes of traffic. She did locate and operate the pedestrian light button and stated that it was time to cross on the basis of stopping perpendicular traffic which did coincide with the pedestrian "go" light. She did not scan for the right-turning cars prior to saying it was safe to cross.

On the opposite side of the street Angela crossed an entrance to a parking lot without scanning and proceeded to locate a grocery store in response to a request. Inside she successfully located several departments and items on request by traveling the periphery of the store. She had difficulty locating chocolate chip cookies before being prompted to scan again and then found them, reading the label. She independently located an open checkout stand and purchased an item appropriately.

When asked to reverse the route and go back to the car, she was hesitant, but with encouragement retraced the first half of the route. On the second half of the route she became disoriented and passed the last turn. With prompts she recovered her orientation and returned successfully.

Summary

Angela is a cooperative, attentive girl. She follows directions well and was a pleasure to work with during the assessment. In spite of her initial uneasiness, she relaxed and performed conscientiously. She has good problem-solving skills and an independent attitude.

Her visual impairment is especially apparent when she is asked to locate and identify objects of various sizes at a distance, such as a fire hydrant, various signs, numbers, and traffic and pedestrian lights. She scans to search for objects, but does not demonstrate safe scanning and related strategies for crossing streets. She has not developed strategies for keeping her orientation in a new environment. She will benefit from orientation and mobility instruction to help her become a safe and increasingly independent traveler.

Recommendations

- Angela will benefit from learning how to use cardinal directions and a compass in travel situations.

- Angela will benefit from learning to use a monocular telescope and/or binoculars to locate and identify/read distant objects/signs, which she can't see with unaided vision.

- Angela will benefit from learning to choose and use landmarks to orient herself and retain orientation when traveling in new environments.

- Angela will benefit from learning to use scanning patterns to increase her safety for making street crossings.

- Angela will benefit from learning safe strategies for crossing a variety of streets, with and without sign and traffic light controls.

- Angela will benefit from learning to identify traffic patterns at intersections to help her to time safe street crossings.

- Angela will benefit from learning to identify and cope with:

  1. Masking sounds (sounds that cover other sounds, such as the noise from an approaching vehicle).

  2. Sound shadows (objects that block sound that is coming from a sound source).

  3. Any object that obscures her view of the street or hides her from the driver's view, such as a parked car, telephone pole, etc.

The orientation and mobility assessment results indicate that Angela's ability to travel safely in the community is affected by her visual impairment.

Natalie Knott
Teacher of Students with Visual Impairment
Orientation and Mobility Specialist

FIGURE 3.4 **Sample O&M Assessment Report** (continued)

The Individualized Education Program

Once the orientation and mobility (O&M) specialist has developed a picture of a student's current travel skills and need for O&M instruction, it is time to develop a plan for instruction. As described in Chapter 1, the Individuals with Disabilities Education Act (IDEA) mandates that all students with disabilities, including those with visual impairments, have an Individualized Education Program (IEP) (or an Individualized Family Service Plan [IFSP] for infants). The visible evidence of such a plan is a written document that includes vital information regarding the student's physical status and present levels of educational performance and the services that are planned for him or her. (See Figure 4.1 for a sample of Part I of an IEP form.) Each school district may have its own form for recording students' IEPs, but the content to be included is generally the same.

The IEP includes the following information for each of the student's areas of need:

- annual educational goals

- short-term objectives

- criteria for evaluating the achievement of these goals and objectives

- proposed possible achievement dates

OCEANA UNIFIED SCHOOL DISTRICT

Part I
Page _1_ of ___

INDIVIDUALIZED EDUCATION PROGRAM

Meeting Date

Initial Entry Date | Next Review Date | Next 3 Year Evaluation Date

Purpose of Meeting: (✓ all that apply)
❐ INITIAL ❐ INTERIM
❐ ANNUAL ❐ NEW TO DISTRICT
❐ ADDENDUM to IEP dated: ________
❐ EXIT
❐ TRIENNIAL/3 YEAR REVIEW

Name: ________ Social Security Number: ________ Sex: ____
Birthdate: ______ Grade: ____ Ethnicity: ______ Primary Language: ______ LEP ❐ Yes ❐ No Residential Status: ____
Student Address: ________ Telephone: (___)______
Street City State Zip Code
Attendance School: ________ Residence School: ________ (If different from residence school, explain why)________

❐ Parent (10) ❐ Guardian (10) ❐ Foster (30) ❐ Surrogate (10) ❐ Other (90) ❐ CASR (10) ❐ LCI (20) ❐ Ward of Court (20)
Name of Care Provider: ________

Parent/Guardian Name | Home Telephone | Work Telephone | Emergency Telephone
Address: ________

ELIGIBILITY FOR SPECIAL EDUCATION: ❐ Eligible Primary Handicapping Condition: ________ ❐ Not Eligible

SPECIFIC LEARNING DISABILITY: Basic Psychological Processing Disorder(s) causing a discrepancy in the areas identified below: (✓ all that apply)

Psychological/Cognitive Processes:
❐ Auditory Processing ❐ Association
❐ Visual Processing ❐ Conceptualization
❐ Sensory-Motor Skills ❐ Expression
❐ Attention

Academic Areas:
❐ Basic Reading Skills ❐ Written Language
❐ Reading Comprehension ❐ Math Reasoning
❐ Listening Comprehension ❐ Math Calculation
❐ Oral Expression

SLD eligibility requires that the following statements are valid:
❐ The discrepancy is not due to factors of environment, cultural differences or econom
❐ The discrepancy is not the result of visual, hearing or motor disability, mental retard
❐ The discrepancy cannot be accommodated through other regular or categorical servi

Recommended Program	Subject Area	Person Responsible	Location (type of instructional room)
❐ General Education Class			
❐ Resource Specialist (420)			
❐ Special Day Class (430) ❐ NSH ❐ SH			
❐ Non-Public School (440)			
❐ Speech (50)			
Physical Education ❐ Regular ❐ Modified ❐ APE			

Part I
Page _2_ of ___

INDIVIDUALIZED EDUCATION PROGRAM

Student Name: ________ Birthdate: ________ Meeting Date: ________

Supplemental aides and services needed to participate in general education program: ________

Assistive Services: (List special materials and equipment and identify in IEP Part II, Standards and Benchmarks)________

Low Incidence: ❐ Yes ❐ No Eligibility Area: ________

1. ____% of time in special education classroom ____% of time in regular classroom. 2. ❐ Recess/Break with General Ed. Population ❐ Lunch with General Education Students ❐ School-wide Activities

3. Explanation of the time when the student <u>will not</u> participate in the general education program:

'egarding child's education: ________

❐ Yes ❐ No
lowing reasons:

Transportation
❐ District
❐ Reimbursement
❐ Tickets
❐ AC
❐ Bart

/Language: (✓ all that apply)
'es ❐ No If yes, identify linguistically and culturally
rds and Benchmarks in IEP Part II and complete/attach
nation Sheet.
aring: ❐ Yes ❐ No If yes, identify linguistically and
ate Standards and Benchmarks in IEP Part II.
node: (✓ all that apply)
❐ Total Communication ❐ Other (explain)

iat apply)
d: ❐ Yes ❐ No Blind: ❐ Yes ❐ No
❐ Yes ❐ No Enlarged Print: ❐ Yes ❐ No
n: ❐ Yes ❐ No

Intervention Plan:
impedes his/her learning and/or learning of others:
❐ Yes ❐ No
'ioral plan and identify in IEP Part II, Standards and

STANDARDS FOR STATE/DISTRICT ASSESSMENTS:
(Choose one)
1. ❐ Regular Test, no accommodations
❐ Regular Test with the following accommodations: ____

OR:
2. ❐ Partial Test: (✓ all that apply)
❐ Reading ❐ Math ❐ Writing
❐ History ❐ Social Science ❐ Science

OR:
3. ❐ Alternative Test(s) (specify): ________

OR:
4. ❐ Not applicable: (preschool/kindergarten or 12th grade only)

Transition Services: (choose one and explain)
❐ Pre-school to elementary: ________
❐ Special Ed. to General Ed.: ________
❐ Elementary to Middle School or Middle to High School: ________
❐ Age 14 or older, (Identify in IEP Part III Individual Transition Plan, (ITP):
❐ Not Applicable (explanation): ________

WHITE – SPECIAL EDUCATION FILE ● GREEN – MIS ● YELLOW – SCHOOL FILE ● PINK – PARENT ● GOLDENROD - TEACHER

Part I
Page _3_ of ___

INDIVIDUALIZED EDUCATION PROGRAM

Student Name: ________ Birthdate: ________ Meeting Date: ________

Progress Reports: How and when student's parents will be informed of progress toward annual goals:
General Education Report Card: ❐ Yes ❐ No If no, rationale: ________
AND/OR
IEP Part II, Standards and Benchmarks: Frequency: ❐ Quarterly ❐ Trimester ❐ Semester ❐ Other
Modified Grades: ❐ Yes ❐ No (If yes, rationale described in IEP Team meeting notes)

DISTRICT PROMOTION/RETENTION STANDARDS
(Choose one)
❐ District Standards
❐ District Standards w/accommodations (identify):
❐ IEP Team determined Standards (if checked, promotion criteria described in IEP Team meeting notes and identified in IEP Part II, Standards and Benchmarks.

Rights Transfer:
Student is 17 years of age ❐ Yes ❐ No
❐ If yes, student has been informed of his/her rights and that they transfer to him/her at the age of majority (18 under California law). ______ Student Initials

WORKABILITY SERVICES:
(Secondary only)
Student receives Workability Services: ❐ Yes ❐ No
If yes, refer to IEP Part III (ITP) and IEP Part II, Standards and Benchmarks. Rationale: ________

HIGH SCHOOL EXIT EXAMINATION
❐ Regular test (for diploma) ❐ Parent/Student notified of required pending examination ______ Parent Initials
❐ Regular test (for diploma) with the following accommodations (identify): ________
❐ Alternative Assessment(s): (identified in IEP Team meeting notes)
❐ Certificate of Completion: (rationale identified in IEP Team meeting notes)

PARENT APPROVAL AND INFORMED CONSENT:
❐ I have been informed of my rights as the parent of a student with special education needs.
❐ I agree with this Individualized Education Program and the placement recommendation(s).
❐ I only agree with implementation of the following parts of the IEP (explanation in IEP Team meeting notes).
PARENT/GUARDIAN SIGNATURE* ________ DATE: ________

IEP TEAM

SIGNATURE*	TITLE	DATE	SIGNATURE	TITLE	DATE
	Administrator/Designee				
	Special Education Teacher				
	General Education Teacher				
	Student (if appropriate)				

* Dissenting team members write "dissent" by name and attach explanation in IEP Team meeting notes.

DISTRIBUTION: ● WHITE – SPECIAL EDUCATION FILE ● GREEN – MIS ● YELLOW – SCHOOL FILE ● PINK – PARENT ● GOLDENROD - TEACHER

FIGURE 4.1 Sample IEP Form

- types and levels of educational services that the student is designated to receive

- frequency and total amount of time for each type of service

- special materials and equipment that the student requires to fulfill his or her educational plan

Figure 4.2 shows a sample page from Part II of the IEP of Angela Uribe, the student whose O&M assessment report was presented in Chapter 3. This form shows Angela's present level of achievement in one O&M area, street crossing, based on this assessment, as well as the goal and objectives.

The IEP document is written, reviewed, and revised by the members of an IEP team, consisting of various individuals who are involved with the student and his or her education. Team members may represent several disciplines, such as speech and language therapy, occupational therapy, physical therapy, and augmentative communication. The parents or guardian, teacher of students with visual impairments, and O&M specialist are also present, as are the student's general education teacher and administrators. For example:

> Janine, an elementary student with multiple and visual impairments, is to be placed in a special class for students with visual impairments. She receives the additional services of a speech and language specialist, an occupational therapist, and an O&M specialist. Her primary placement will be with the teacher of students with visual impairments in a special class with other students who are visually impaired. As the case manager, this teacher coordinates the IEP meetings. The IEP team also consists of Janine's mother and father, the speech and language specialist, the occupational therapist, the classroom teacher, Janine's social worker, the school principal, and a special education administrator.

The written IEP plan that is eventually produced has to be signed by all the team members at an IEP meeting before it goes into effect. Subsequent IEP meetings may be convened by any member of the team to address important issues that arise or to effect changes in the plan regarding goals, objectives, types and levels of service, or amounts of service time.

IEP PART II: STANDARDS (GOALS) AND BENCHMARKS (OBJECTIVES)

Student _Angela Uribe_ School _M. L. King Middle School_ Meeting Date _12/14/02_ _Orientation & Mobility Specialist_

Reviewer/Evaluator of IEP

Area of Need: ☐ Academic ☐ Social/Emotional ☐ Pre-Vocational/Vocational ☐ Communication ☐ Behavioral ☐ Perceptual/motor ☒ Other _Orientation & Mobility_

Present Level of Performance: Data must include strengths, needs, involvement in the general education (core) curriculum, and observations.

Angela follows directions well. She demonstrates some strategies and practices for deciding when it is safe to cross a street. She scans but does not use a patterned nor complete scan consistently. She lacks skills for preparing for and timing a safe street crossing.

Standard: Annual Standard (Goal) and Benchmarks (Objectives) must relate to student's needs to enable the student to be involved and progress in the general education (core) curriculum.

Angela will demonstrate the ability to plan and make safe street crossings at a variety of intersections.

Benchmark/Short-Term Objective and Mastery Criteria: *Angela will demonstrate knowledge of the safest place to stand when planning a street crossing.* By date: _4/03_ with _100_ % accuracy	Evaluation Method TO DC	Date 4/03 Prog. Rpt.	Date 6/03 Prog. Rpt.	Date 11/03 Prog. Rpt.	Date 1/04 Prog. Rpt.
Benchmark/Short-Term Objective and Mastery Criteria: *Angela will demonstrate the use of scanning patterns to make safe street crossings.* By date: _6/03_ with _100_ % accuracy	Evaluation Method TO DC	Date 4/03 Prog. Rpt.	Date 6/03 Prog. Rpt.	Date 11/03 Prog. Rpt.	Date 1/04 Prog. Rpt.
Benchmark/Short-Term Objective and Mastery Criteria: By date: _____ with _____ % accuracy	Evaluation Method	Date Prog. Rpt.	Date Prog. Rpt.	Date Prog. Rpt.	Date Prog. Rpt.

*TO = teacher observation   DC = data collection

FIGURE 4.2 Sample O&M IEP

PREPARING FOR THE IEP MEETING

Before a finished document can be produced, recorded, and signed, there is a lot of work to be done. Information-gathering and assessment procedures, like those discussed in Chapter 3, create the groundwork upon which the IEP is built.

Each team member who represents a discipline whose services address the student's assessed needs proceeds along a parallel course, eventually producing a section of the document with its respective goals and objectives. The team specialists, including the O&M specialist, each prepare an assessment report for newly referred students or an annual report for continuing students, like the O&M assessment report for Angela shown in Figure 3.4 in Chapter 3. The team members also develop statements regarding the student's present level of skills in their respective disciplines and propose goals and objectives.

Establishing the Meeting Date

When many individuals are involved in the educational planning and provision of services for a student, it is up to the case manager—in Janine's case, the teacher of students with visual impairments—to check with all the team members to establish the most convenient time to meet. The case manager then uses a written form to notify them all of the meeting time, date, and place. It is advisable to take the initiative to check with the case manager periodically about when he or she anticipates scheduling the IEP meeting for a particular student, even though in some cases the date may be only approximate. It is a good idea to note this date on an IEP calendar (see Figure 2.6 in Chapter 2) and to check with the meeting coordinator periodically until a date is finalized. Otherwise, you may get lost in the shuffle and fail to be notified of the meeting.

Consultation and Goal Preparation

In preparing the O&M goals, the O&M specialist works closely with the parent or guardian and student, as appropriate, to learn about their concerns and the goals they wish the student to achieve. For example, a mother may desire that her son learn his way around the neighborhood park, with an emphasis on using the slide and swings independently. A teenage girl may wish to learn to use public transportation so she does not have to take the schoolbus.

It may be advisable for the O&M specialist to set up a meeting with the family prior to the formal IEP meeting to provide a forum for voicing the family's concerns before the IEP goals are written. This meeting may be held at school or in the student's home. Students may be involved to the degree that their awareness and sense of responsibility enable them to participate in and profit from the experience. It is essential that, when possible, students are active participants in helping to establish the goals that will shape their lives. They need to be the subjects, not the objects, of the IEPs.

At such meetings, family members may voice their hopes, fears, and doubts. It is important that the O&M specialist conduct the meeting with sensitivity so as to allow the participants to express their underlying concerns freely, as in the following situation:

> The parents of Christina, a sheltered 13-year-old girl who was visually impaired, decided that it was important that she learn to make safe street crossings at a busy light-controlled intersection in their neighborhood after their older daughter had been injured by a car at the same intersection. This was a commendable decision, given what the IEP team observed was the parents' propensity to overprotect. The parents' decision was motivated by common sense and the fear that Christina might meet with a fate similar to her sister's.
>
> In this situation, Christina's usual yearning for increased independence was sharply curtailed by her fear of being hit by a vehicle. During the pre-IEP meeting, it was necessary to uncover and explore this fear and its effect on her motivation. The O&M specialist was able to reassure Christina by promising that she would use a slow and gradual approach toward attaining the goal if it was deemed appropriate in the final analysis. It would have been inappropriate to adopt this particular street-crossing goal for Christina without her agreement.

If, for some reason, it is not possible for the O&M specialist to meet with the parents before the IEP meeting or even to consult by telephone about their goals, the specialist may come to the meeting with tentative goals that the family and other team members can discuss and modify as necessary.

WRITING IEPS

The O&M specialist is responsible for completing O&M goals and objectives in Part II of the IEP. The IEP can be part of a blueprint for the student's O&M instruction, since it provides a reference point from which to chart your direction when planning lessons. Only key goals are delineated in the IEP, although related goals are covered during lesson periods. The Checklist of Orientation and Mobility Instructional Areas and Related Objectives (which appears in the Appendix to this book) provides lists of potential target skills in the various areas of the O&M curriculum. This checklist may be used in conjunction with assessment findings and other checklists to isolate goals and objectives and create a comprehensive plan that includes goals and objectives not written in the IEP. The specific goals and objectives that are included for a particular student may be expanded and personalized to reflect his or her individual needs.

There are three major sections in this part of the IEP. Although the specific structure and components of the IEP vary from school district to school district, all IEPs contain—for each area of need—the *present level of performance* or educational attainment, *long-term goals or standards,* and *short-term objectives or benchmarks*, as shown in the example of Angela's IEP presented in Figure 4.2 and another page of her IEP shown in Figure 4.3. There may be a different page of goals and objectives for every general area of the O&M curriculum.

Present Level of Performance

The present level of performance section of the IEP describes the student's current performance in a particular area of need. It presents strengths, weaknesses, educational progress, and present conditions related to the student. When writing up present levels,

- be sure that all statements are accurate, being derived from direct observations and assessment results and described in *measurable* terms and in *everyday language;*

- document both strengths and weaknesses, maintaining a positive tone without sacrificing honesty;

- state which prior goals have been attained or not attained;

IEP PART II: STANDARDS (GOALS) AND BENCHMARKS (OBJECTIVES)

Student __Angela Uribe__   School __M. L. King Middle School__   Meeting Date __12/14/02__   __Orientation & Mobility Specialist__

Reviewer/Evaluator of IEP

Area of Need: ☐ Academic ☐ Social/Emotional ☐ Pre-Vocational/Vocational ☐ Communication ☐ Behavioral ☐ Perceptual/motor ☒ Other __Orientation & Mobility__

Present Level of Performance: Data must include strengths, needs, involvement in the general education (core) curriculum, and observations.

Angela demonstrates many age-appropriate skills with regard to body image; laterality; quantitative, directional, and positional concepts; personal information, and on-campus orientation & mobility. She demonstrates needs in the area of distance vision use because she is unable to locate and identify objects and read signs at a distance.

Standard: Annual Standard (Goal) and Benchmarks (Objectives) must relate to student's needs to enable the student to be involved and progress in the general education (core) curriculum.

Angela will demonstrate the ability to use aids to increase her vision use at a distance.

Benchmark/Short-Term Objective and Mastery Criteria:

Angela will focus a monocular/binoculars on a stationary object from a stationary position.

By date: __4/03__ with __100__ % accuracy

Evaluation Method	Date 4/03	Date 6/03	Date 11/03	Date 1/04
TO DC	Prog. Rpt.	Prog. Rpt.	Prog. Rpt.	Prog. Rpt.

Benchmark/Short-Term Objective and Mastery Criteria:

Angela will use a monocular/binoculars to locate an object from an array of objects or complex background, for example, signs, house number, traffic and pedestrian lights.

By date: __6/03__ with __100__ % accuracy

Evaluation Method	Date 4/03	Date 6/03	Date 11/03	Date 1/04
TO DC	Prog. Rpt.	Prog. Rpt.	Prog. Rpt.	Prog. Rpt.

Benchmark/Short-Term Objective and Mastery Criteria:

By date: _____ with _____ % accuracy

Evaluation Method	Date	Date	Date	Date
	Prog. Rpt.	Prog. Rpt.	Prog. Rpt.	Prog. Rpt.

*TO = teacher observation   DC = data collection

FIGURE 4.3 Sample O&M IEP Goals and Objectives

- report the lack of expected progress and suspected reasons; and

- include a statement regarding the student's need for supplemental aids, such as a long cane.

In Figure 4.3, the O&M specialist reports on Angela's level of attainment in skills related to body image concepts and in using her distance vision, based on the assessment reported in Figure 3.4.

Annual Goals

Annual goals relate to the student's needs as described in the present level of performance. These are goals that the student can reasonably accomplish in a year, and they must be measurable. When writing annual goals,

- target essential areas of instruction, derived from the present-level section;

- keep the goal statements short and general;

- keep the time frame in mind and include only those goals that can be realistically addressed; and

- present goals in specific terms.

An example of an annual goal for Angela that meets these criteria is "Angela will focus a monocular/bionoculars on a stationary object from a stationary position by April 2003 with 100% accuracy."

Short-Term Instructional Objectives

Annual goals are broken down into short-term objectives or benchmarks, by which progress toward the goal can be measured. Short-term instructional objectives must include the following information:

- who is being evaluated

- the activity or skill to be performed and to what degree of accuracy

- the context in which the skill or activity is performed

- by what date

- measured by what criteria

Thus, an appropriate short-term objective for Angela, based on the annual goal in Figure 4.3, is "Angela will use a monocular/binoculars to locate an object from an array of objects or complex background by June 2003 (the next progress report date), with 100% accuracy, as measured by the teacher's observation and data collection." The IEP includes space to provide a progress report for each short-term objective at regular intervals.

Bear in mind that if a student is moving to a new site, the travel goals that a student has achieved at the present site may not be generalized and will need to be extended and worked on anew at the unfamiliar site. In addition, accomplished goals may not be retained over prolonged vacations and may need to be extended into the new term.

Duration of Goals and Objectives

The IEP goals and objectives provide a reference point for the ensuing educational planning and resultant lessons. They do not, however, constitute an inflexible document cast in concrete, rigidly regulating all processes. When goals are rapidly attained or prove to be inappropriate, they may be rewritten. If goals are not attained within the projected time frame, they may be extended when appropriate.

THE IEP MEETING

The IEP is a joint production of the parents, the student (if appropriate), administrators, and the entire educational team. The present levels of performance and the goals from each discipline, including O&M, are reviewed with the entire group at the meeting for discussion of suggestions, changes, additions, and deletions.

Transdisciplinary Goals

The IEP meeting provides an excellent opportunity for targeting appropriate inter- and transdisciplinary goals that all members of the student's broader support team—defined as all the significant individuals who come into repeated contact with the student in the course of the student's daily life—can adopt and carry out on a global level (see the section on the Support Team in Chapter 9). For example, the speech therapist may want the student to learn to communicate in complete sentences. The O&M specialist may want the student to learn to open doors. The classroom teacher may want the student to learn to ask for help when she cannot do something. The parents may want the student to learn to stop whining. When all members of the support team are aware of these goals, they can combine their efforts to reinforce or extinguish targeted behaviors.

If for some reason all goals are not reviewed at the IEP meeting, or if you are unable to attend, it is a good idea to get a copy of the entire IEP and isolate the goals that may be translated into common goals across the disciplines. These common goals can be incorporated, when it is natural and convenient to do so, into your lesson time with the student.

Putting the Document into Effect

At the end of the IEP meeting, the participants come to an agreement on the student's placement, the support services he or she needs to receive, and the proposed goals and objectives in each discipline. Once everyone signs the signature page, the document goes into effect. If there is any disagreement, the document may be renegotiated on the spot or at another meeting in the future. When complete, all parts of the IEP, including the present levels, goals, and objectives, are assembled, and the copies are distributed to all participants and any other service providers according to the regulations governing their distribution.

As noted, the IEP provides an outline of some important general goals and specific objectives for students. The O&M specialist will be making detailed plans for instruction based not only on each student's IEP and the assessment of needs, but on his or her knowledge of teaching young people. The following chapter discusses approaches to teaching O&M to young students who are visually impaired.

Approaches
to Teaching O&M

Teaching orientation and mobility (O&M) to children and adolescents is most successful when the O&M instructor can cultivate an environment that is supportive of learning for his or her students. Young O&M students have different needs than do adult learners, and they approach their task with a more limited understanding of their environment and the importance of learning O&M skills. To create the conditions that best facilitate O&M instruction, the instructor needs to:

- understand young students and how they learn best
- help students develop a broad base of knowledge of a range of concepts
- use language that will be most effective with students
- stimulate students' desire to learn
- ensure students' basic comfort and safety

These essential topics are explored in this chapter.

TEACHING YOUNG PEOPLE

It is important to recognize that young students can differ from adults in significant ways that must be taken into consideration when working with them. The younger the students are, the more true the following generalizations about young learners will be for them:

- They may have an abundance of energy. It is helpful to provide outlets for this energy during lessons or to channel it in productive ways.

- They tend to be process, rather than product, oriented. Therefore, the process of learning must be compelling in itself because the product—such as "safe travel" or "consistent hazard detection"—is likely to be abstract and unreal to them and will not serve as a motivator.

- They tend to respond to concrete, rather than abstract, methods of teaching and benefit from "hands-on" experience-based learning situations—all the more so when they have little or no vision.

- They commonly have a strong hunger for novelty and amusement. It is important to present lessons in fresh and amusing ways.

You can be fairly sure that if the teacher feels bored with what and how he or she is teaching, the student will be bored as well and therefore less inclined to learn. The section on Building Motivation, Using Imagination later in this chapter provides suggestions for promoting students' interest and explores ways to deal with abundant energy and flagging attention. And, as emphasized throughout this chapter, it is important to get to know individual students to find out what sparks their interest or captures their imagination.

TEACHING CONCEPTS

Young people who are visually impaired or blind differ from their adult counterparts in other ways as well. Adults who become O&M students usually arrive on the scene with a vast accumulation of knowledge about the world around them that they have gained simply by virtue of the experience that has accrued with age. They have had a lifetime of opportunity to form concepts—generalized mental representations or understanding about their environment and the way the world is structured. This is especially true of those who became adventitiously blind as adults or who have lost sight gradually from a prior state of intact vision. These individuals have experiential and conceptual development that is on a par with that of the majority of the population who have intact vision. Adults who have had some form of visual impairment from birth or early childhood also may have developed sound conceptual knowledge, as well as compensatory skills and adaptive behaviors, as a result of their life experiences and previous special education and training. By and large, then, adults who are O&M students have a foundation of conceptual knowledge that facilitates their learning of travel skills.

By contrast, young people who are visually impaired or blind who become O&M students present unique challenges with respect to learning travel skills because they frequently lack this conceptual foundation. People with intact vision develop knowledge about many areas—such as their bodies, their environment, physical relationships, and movement—almost unconsciously as a result of having unfettered access to visual information. The capacity to interact with the world visually confers rapid access to information that would take an enormous amount of time to access tactilely or through other senses and might not be readily understandable even then, without an accompanying verbal explanation. Yet many of these concepts are fundamental to learning travel skills, so it is the responsibility of the O&M specialist to help students understand them.

Basic O&M Concepts

The term *concept* is a deceptively small word that, when used to refer to teaching and practicing O&M, covers an enormous array of ideas that touch on most aspects of life. Sidebar 5.1 lists categories and subcategories of the concepts that are basic to O&M. Young people who are congenitally visually impaired or blind need to learn about these concepts and related information as a basis for understanding the world around them. Moreover, helping them develop a conceptual foundation is fundamental to learning travel skills.

A teacher may feel overwhelmed by the breadth and magnitude of these concepts when thinking about how to teach them to students who are blind, but taking a systematic approach to selecting the focus of your lessons can make this task manageable. Although it is beyond the scope of this work to present a comprehensive catalog of these items or exhaustive instructions for teaching them, Fazzi and Petersmeyer (2001) set forth a variety of means for teaching concepts in

---

SIDEBAR 5.1 **Categories of Basic O&M Concepts**

The following categories and subcategories are concepts that are fundamental to learning orientation and travel skills and that need to be learned as part of the O&M curriculum.

- Body Concepts
    - body parts
    - planes
    - body movement
    - laterality
    - directionality
- Spatial Concepts
    - shapes
    - dimension
    - measurement
    - positional/relational
    - action

- Environmental Concepts
    - travel
    - geographic
    - architectural
    - topographic
    - meteorological
    - temperature
    - textural
    - traffic
- Temporal Concepts
    - measurement of time
    - sequencing, as of steps, procedures, and activities

---

an engaging and creative manner. This chapter suggests some starting points for teaching basic O&M concepts, as well as ways to make learning concepts more interesting and meaningful for students. Some additional suggestions appear in the section on teaching orientation skills in Chapter 7.

It is similarly challenging to assess the conceptual knowledge of a student, but formal testing tools and procedures can be a helpful way to start. (See the Resources section for a listing and description of some assessment tools.) It takes time to discern the degree to which a student has generalized a specific concept. This does not occur during a one-time evaluation, but rather during diagnostic teaching—the process of continuous informal assessment that takes place as a teacher instructs a student in a variety of situations and under different circumstances.

Once the initial assessment is complete, it is a good idea to isolate several of the most functional and basic concepts that are weak or lacking and start teaching them. Providing repeated exposure to the concepts in different contexts is necessary for the student to retain and then generalize them.

Generalizing from the Concrete

Learning experiences that are intended to teach concepts are most effective when they help students expand and generalize concrete knowledge they already have about the physical self, how it moves, and the world within which it moves. With young students, teaching often focuses on defining and redefining tangible objects and their properties until the students develop a global understanding of the objects' many facets.

Lessons must also be structured to take nothing for granted. It is important for the O&M specialist to perform frequent "reality checks" to make sure that he or she is communicating in a manner that connects with, and possibly modifies and expands, the student's concept of himself or herself and the world in which the student lives, as shown in the following example:

> Teaching Audra, a sixth-grade student who is blind, what a T-shaped intersection is took time and was approached from several points of view. A T-shaped intersection has a unique physical shape. This shape affects the way cars behave by limiting their travel to specific trajectories governed by traffic laws. A T-shaped intersection also affects the way pedestrians behave by defining their travel as well.
>
> Simply presenting a verbal explanation of this concept could not provide a true definition for Audra when she lacked the requisite foundational knowledge. Audra needed to be shown in concrete terms what a T-shaped intersection is. She needed to know how a "T" is shaped and had to experience movement, as both a pedestrian and a passenger, in all aspects of travel at such an intersection. She did not even know how the print letter "T" is shaped, since the braille representation is very different.
>
> Audra experienced the concept of a T-shaped intersection defined on a variety of levels and from a variety of perspectives. First, her O&M specialist presented her with a tactile alphabet letter card so she could see how a print "T" was shaped. She explored the juncture of the two lines tactilely. Then she worked at constructing a model of a T-shaped intersection using a miniature teacher-made tactile kit similar to a Chang kit. She used her model with miniature cars to replicate traffic flow while listening to the traffic at the intersection.
>
> Audra trailed the sidewalk at the top of the "T" with her

cane. Then she rode in the O&M specialist's car with her model of the intersection and replicated the car's movements with her tiny car, experiencing three approaches to the intersection and the possible trajectories of car movement given the shape of the intersection. Audra also located and explored T-shaped intersections in the halls at her school.

It took a number of lessons in different situations for Audra to develop a working knowledge of this concept. By degrees, she was able to construct a tactile and kinetic concept based on her experience with the models and the actual intersection.

Such concepts may need to be reintroduced at different times during the span of a student's training, since limited or absent vision prevents the concept from being reinforced naturally by visual observation across the spectrum of the student's continuing experience.

False Versus Informed Concepts

The term *concept* also encompasses all the attributes of objects in the concrete world that comprise their meaning and identity. Without knowledge of concepts, words can remain one dimensional, representing concepts with no meaning behind them. An individual's facile use of words that represent concepts may mask, rather than reveal, his or her grasp of meaning, as in the following example:

> Early in my career, I conducted a formal assessment of Gina, a third-grade student who was blind and had mild cerebral palsy. Sometime after the assessment, Gina told me with full confidence that a chair had two legs and then proceeded to show me the evidence by patting the two legs at the front of the chair on which she was sitting. Lacking the easy visual access of those with sight, an access that delivers irrefutable evidence of natural laws, Gina constructed her own image of a chair on the basis of an incompletely tactilely explored model. As a beginning teacher, I was distressed that my student had such a dramatic gap in her conceptual knowledge. This gap had not shown up on the Tactile Analog to the Boehm Test of Basic Concepts! As it turned out, Gina's gaps in knowledge were legion.

Gina seemed to know what a chair was, but her seemingly appropriate use of the term disguised her misunderstanding, a gap that even the assessment had failed to reveal. And Gina was not an isolated case. It is crucial that O&M specialists pay close attention to students' actual grasp of concepts, rather than just their ability to use appropriate terminology.

Experiencing the World Tactilely

In promoting the development of concepts among students, it is important to take a concrete hands-on approach. For many students who are visually impaired or blind, the tactile system is a major learning channel that needs to be filled by touching. As these students develop their understanding of concepts, touching and manipulating, coupled with hearing, is their equivalent of seeing.

Touching must go beyond haphazard collisions or the patterned tapping of canes, however. There is a whole world beyond feeling the tactile impact of a cane and hearing the sound it makes. Exploring this world takes time when a room cannot be assessed with a sweep of the eye, but must be examined tactilely inch by inch.

It is particularly important for students in wheelchairs to have opportunities to explore their environment tactilely, when possible, because the increased isolation resulting from their location in wheelchairs can create a further barrier to tactile encounters with their environment, as it did for Enrique:

> When his O&M instructor asked Enrique, a student who was blind and had quadriplegia, "How big is your house?" Enrique replied, "The couch is not very big." Enrique comprehended the size of his house in terms of the realm of the couch where he spent most of his time while at home.

Familiarizing students in wheelchairs to a room needs to be done in a slow, methodical way. First the periphery is examined and then the inner features of the room, to the degree that each is accessible to a wheelchair. When students have a degree of arm motion and hand use they can touch and experience different shapes and textures that objects present as they move themselves or are pushed around a room. When arm and hand use is limited, they can still be pushed and stopped at each landmark. For example, if a feature of the room is a large wooden chair, the O&M specialist can guide the wheelchair over to it. The specialist can briefly identify the chair verbally, tap it several times to give it an auditory property, and then sit it the chair and say a few words to make the object more concrete by using it in the student's presence.

The opportunity for visually impaired students to explore their environment up close, using all their senses, is crucial for them to develop accurate concepts about the world around them.

Regardless of whether students are in wheelchairs or on their feet, it is part of the O&M specialist's job to bring them into contact with their environment so that they are able to perceive it tactilely and thus form accurate concepts about it.

Promoting Imagery

In teaching concepts, it is necessary to increase the scope of students' imagery—their mental representation of the world. Objects must be touched and manipulated repeatedly to plumb their meaning. Architectural details need to be explored. How tall is a wall? What fills the space above my head? What does a window look like? How can corners stick out and be recessed; how can they be sharp and rounded?

It is impossible for students to comprehend most concepts in a short period or after a single exposure. When a student cannot see, it takes time to comprehend and identify the front and back of a car, inside *and* out, including the front and back doors. It can be mystifying to comprehend what the front and back of a store are when the student is inside of it. It is especially difficult if the student is thinking of the front and back of his or her own body that, as the student moves, are continually changing relationship to objects and *their* fronts and backs, and the relationship changes even more if someone has come along and turned the objects around since the last time the student encountered them. It is enough to make the student feel disoriented! A gradual approach to teaching concepts, presenting many repetitions over time and in a variety of situations, with repeated opportunities for tactile exploration, will yield the most detailed mental image and the most thorough understanding.

Promoting Functionality

To ensure that students generalize and solidify concepts, it is important to adopt a perspective of *functionality*—that is, to show how these things or objects exist in the real world, what they do, and how and why they are used. Concepts need to be taught within the natural flow of living processes.

For example, the word *square* has many meanings. If a student, especially a preschooler or someone with cognitive deficits, has any knowledge of the concept at all, the word *square* by itself, without any referent or context, probably connotes a specific shape and scale associated with other shapes the student has encountered while playing with shape puzzles. However, *square* may also be the shape of a city block, another term for a plaza, an action taken to align two objects, or a type of dance. Each of these meanings of *square* is related to or abstracted from the basic shape that can be learned from a preschooler's puzzle. However, a piece of a puzzle is a far cry from the alignment of two bodies. Focusing abstractly on the properties of the square shape in a different or broader context can be misleading to an inexperienced student.

Teaching concepts in isolation must be approached with discretion and with a view toward supporting their generalization into other spheres of the student's life. With young students and those with cognitive deficits, it is especially important to present concepts in the context of their everyday lives or within the format of games and during the process of play. Thus, a student may be shown square shapes in the environment through a game of "finding squares" of different sizes. Promoting a "concept of the week" (or month) can be a means by which squares can be isolated or presented as they are encountered within the experiences of many different activities. Consequently, learning becomes the by-product of being engaged in an enjoyable or meaningful activity, rather than the focus of an academic exercise.

For many students, isolated drills can be counterproductive to effective learning because they do not appear functional and therefore engender boredom, as in the following example:

When Thomas, an elementary special day student who is blind, was encouraged to practice squaring off repeatedly from an arbitrarily chosen wall in the hall near his classroom, his attention flagged because the experience lacked connection and purpose for him. The skill was being presented in isolation. In an effort to motivate Thomas, the O&M specialist coupled this practice with a game of square and shoot, in which Thomas had to square to the wall and retain this position to shoot a ball accurately to a silent partner. Once he began playing the game, Thomas became engaged and motivated because he was having fun. His activity had immediate rewards.

Thomas also learned the functionality of squaring off when traveling the route from the bus to his classroom in the morning. If he did not square off accurately, he lost alignment for crossing open spaces and might lose his way and be late for class—a natural and negative consequence for him. When Thomas had to square off within the framework of a functional daily route, both motivation and repetitions were built into a naturally goal-directed process.

In contrast to a young student such as Thomas, who needed the incentive of a game to motivate him to practice, an older student with greater maturity, experience, and depth of conceptual knowledge would be more likely to be able to benefit from being taught to square off through drill in isolation. Such a student would be capable of generalizing beyond the drill experience to relate it functionally to his or her travel needs in real life.

The Individual Approach

With concepts, as with anything else, students learn eagerly when their unique interests and abilities are encouraged. Taking into consideration their ages and developmental levels; interacting with, observing, and questioning the students themselves; and questioning their parents and other teachers and specialists about them are good ways to find out what motivates and interests them and what has worked in the past. In addition, discerning their evolving gifts and personality traits can be an ongoing and fruitful process when an open-minded and eclectic approach is taken by the teacher, as in this example:

> Although some preschoolers readily participate in body-parts games involving songs and different objects, such as feather dusters, beanbags, or fluorescent stickers, that are used to locate the body parts, Joey shows no interest in such games. However, in a totally different context, he will put Play-Doh (of all things!) on different body parts on request. Similarly, some students eagerly begin to learn a variety of spatial concepts, such as forward, backward, right, left, around, up, and down, while dancing to music. With Faith, however, facings are taught by positioning her in reference to a pile of enormous pillows and rewarding the correct response to commands, such as "about-face" or "quarter turn to the left," with a plunge into the pillows.
>
> Joey shuns such activities, but is intensely responsive to learning spatial concepts within the context of a walk in the park, where the rewards are in the form of hills to go *up* and *down*. Here terms of laterality can take on special significance when the big swings are *to the right* and the rocking lion is *to the left*. When

Joey is allowed to take control and issue the directions—for example, when "Let's go to the right" results in arriving at his favorite destination, the big swings—he is not only rewarded but empowered by the correct use of a term of laterality.

Because many of the fundamental concepts necessary for O&M skills are difficult for visually impaired youngsters to grasp in passing, teaching them requires considerable patience as well as ingenuity by the O&M specialist. Taking the time to allow the student to explore objects and environments thoroughly and repeatedly is an important part of the process, but the learning experience will be most successful when the O&M specialist pays attention to the individual student and what motivates him or her and makes sure the concepts are related to the student's actual experience of the world. One way of making sure that instruction relates to students' own experiences is to use language that is meaningful to them.

THE USE OF LANGUAGE

Teaching relies on our ability to communicate with our students, and the use of language is, of course, central to communication. In communicating with students, achieving understanding depends upon the quantity and quality of the words we couple with modeled behavior and hands-on experience. The way language is used can affect the way students respond to instruction:

- Students respond to instructions delivered in their vernacular.

- Students respond to the introduction of new concepts when these concepts are presented in concrete language that relates to their prior experience.

- Students respond when their imaginations are engaged.

With preschool students, in particular, learning language and learning concepts go hand in hand. Because concepts are, in a sense, mental representations of the world, learning concepts involves learning the language used to represent them. For young children, then, concepts are the substance of concrete language. Playing with language—for example, making up and singing songs that celebrate the activities in which a child is engaged—such as walking *up* and *down* hills or swinging *backward* and *forward* and *faster* and *higher*—can be a delightful and memorable way to begin to couple words with their meanings.

Speaking Their Language

As adults, we have developed rich and complex vocabularies that are the result of much experience and schooling. Students who are visually impaired or blind often lack vocabulary, as well as concepts, by virtue of their impairment, age, inexperience, degree of overprotectedness, and/or cognitive deficits. Interacting with students during the assessment period and initial lessons gives some sense of the range of their vocabulary. As a teacher working with students, it is important to strive to communicate in terms that they will understand, even in regard to the most mundane, everyday expressions, as the following example illustrates:

> A student teacher asked Kurt, to whom she was teaching cane travel, to "walk at a comfortable pace." When the supervising O&M instructor asked the student teacher to question Kurt regarding his understanding of the phrase, Kurt said that he did not know what she meant. Neither did the supervisor. When the student teacher explained her phrase, it turned out that she wanted Kurt to walk faster.

Terms that slip naturally from our tongues may sound like a foreign language to our students.

It is also important to isolate regional and ethnic terminology for various objects, as is evident in the case of Michael:

> I labored in the dark as I struggled to teach concepts related to urban travel to Michael, a high school student with low vision, until I discovered that for him the appropriate name for a street corner was *block*. He and his friends waited for each other "on the block." When I spoke of going "around the block," Michael thought of going around the corner.

Although we were using the same word, we were speaking different languages.

When O&M specialists graduate from their university O&M programs, they have at their disposal a wealth of subject-specific vocabulary related to the field. Using this vocabulary facilitates communication with other O&M specialists. To others, it may be viewed as jargon. To students, without the appropriate introduction, it may be a foreign language that obscures, rather than clarifies, meaning.

For example, when teaching beginning residential-area travel, it can be helpful to refer to *parallel* and *perpendicular* streets as *beside* and *in front* streets, since the latter terms are fundamental in the hierarchy of concept development and are more likely to be understood and generalized by the student. *In front* and *beside* also more readily convey a location that is relative to the student's position when he or she changes direction. Even with students to whom you have introduced the terminology of *parallel* and *perpendicular*, it is a good idea to pair the complex with the simple, referring to "the parallel or *beside* street" until the student can confidently use the geometric term to label the street.

Using Functional Labels

A significant part of human communication is nonverbal. Students who are blind or visually impaired miss aspects of communication that are nonverbal, such as body language, with its full array of eye movements, facial expressions, body movements, and body positions. They also may not see significant "props," such as objects that the teacher may be holding up or a display temporarily arranged at a specific work station in the room. Lacking visual clues, such as the teacher's gesture or directed gaze, makes them more reliant on the detailed verbal information that specific labels impart.

It is advisable to give objects verbal, symbolic, or sign language labels according to the student's unique mode of communication. These labels should describe objects and/or denote their functions or locations. Using specific, functional labels avoids the confusion that generic labels, such as "table," can generate, since there can be many tables in the classroom, and promotes orientation. A label should designate the object in a manner that reflects its function, and it is important that all the members of the student's support team (see Chapter 9) use the label appropriately and consistently.

For example, if there is more than one large table in the classroom, each should be labeled differently, such as "snack table," "work table," and so forth. If there is more than one door in the room, they also should be appropriately labeled, such as "hall door," "outside door," and "closet door." Similarly, hallways in schools should be designated by terms like "main hall," "upper-" and "lower-grade" halls, and "library hall." Designating halls by a numbering system is appropriate for those with the associated developmental and cognitive abilities. Designations may change as the student matures. Doors may also be labeled "push" and "pull" doors or "doorknob doors." The right and left sides of "push" and "pull" doors may be labeled *hinge* and *open* sides. Students who are blind often struggle with attempting to push a door open from the side closest to the hinges. This, of course, is a losing battle. Prompting them to locate and identify the *open* side of the door facilitates their opening it.

The Fuel of Imagination

It is also a good idea to use language that gets a student's attention by engaging his or her imagination. For example, presenting an O&M lesson to fourth grader Todd in terms of an adventure in which he, as an explorer, creates a map of a foreign, imaginary, or extraterrestrial territory promotes a peak learning experience. Given that context, Todd operates on a level of excited involvement while drawing and labeling such mundane things as streets and landmarks.

Students can find the use of personifications engaging. Some students spontaneously give names to their canes. For example, upon receiving a new cane, Joel, an elementary school student, named it Curbie, explaining that it helped him to locate curbs. The name graduated to each new cane as Joel grew during a period of eight years. Other ways to capture students' imaginations and encourage them to be involved in the learning process are discussed in the next section.

BUILDING MOTIVATION, USING IMAGINATION

Creativity, Imagination, and Play

As previously discussed with regard to teaching concepts and the use of language, the learning process is greatly enhanced when students' imaginations are engaged and their interests are harnessed. Students need to be challenged to learn, and external incentives enhance the process of learning and make it memorable. Boredom is a great enemy of learning, whereas novelty and opportunities for spontaneity infuse times of learning with fascination and fun. Keeping this point in mind—as well as the fact that, as Ralph Waldo Emerson said, "a foolish consistency is the hobgoblin of little minds"—teachers will be less likely to hold to endless repetitions of the tried and true. Engaging a student's interest consistently provides the greatest fuel for learning.

The mastery of O&M skills and the greater freedom that a student experiences as he or she becomes a competent traveler are potent incentives by themselves, especially for older students. When dealing with the difficult and sometimes tedious details of learning cane techniques and the whole range of orientation skills, however, the additional motivators of play, fun, excitement, or intrigue may be necessary, especially with students who are young and those with developmental disabilities.

When students have fun on mobility lessons, they will look forward to them with a pleasant sense of anticipation. When fun is interwoven with work, they will readily tackle tasks that are focused on learning new skills. The students in the following example enjoy their walk so much that they do not realize that they are working hard:

> Denise and Terin, two visually impaired elementary school students, happily practice a variety of cane skills on the route to the pine cone tree that stands at the far margin of the schoolyard between the school and the community. The tree signals the decline of a steep hill. It is the home of birds and sheds pine cones in all seasons. Denise and Terin never tire of traveling there to search for pine cones, practicing cane techniques to locate them. The terrain is hilly and uneven, covered with grass, pine needles, and ivy and woven throughout with knobby roots. Sometimes they find other objects: a blue T-shirt, a pair of Groucho Marx glasses, a fragrant pine branch, or a small eraser shaped like a car.
>
> One day when Terin and I reached the pine cone tree on our way into the community, a mockingbird perched above us was singing loudly. Terin set his cane down and extracted a harmonica from his pocket. He lifted his head toward the branches and played a few notes. The bird hushed. Terin played again and then stopped. The brief silence was punctuated by a burst of bird song. Terin threw his head back in a sneeze of laughter and blew into the harmonica. The bird, in turn, became silent. When Terin stopped, the bird answered with a stream of song. At the conclusion of the duet, we proceeded down the steep hill, working on detecting the up-and-down contours of the driveways that regularly punctuated the steep sidewalk.

Maintaining an atmosphere that allows for the unexpected and takes advantage of it permits students to be spontaneous and to express themselves in creative ways. This makes for motivating and memorable lesson periods.

Keep in mind, as you plan lessons for your students, that learning O&M skills happens while students are participating in other meaningful activities. It happens on the way to the school cafeteria or supermarket, on the playground, and at the park. It happens while shopping at the mall or on a trip to the barber shop. It happens between memorable events. It is the concomitant of exploratory play and meaningful activity. Sometimes it is one and the same.

Games and Adventures

If teachers permit themselves to get in touch with their youthful selves and give free rein to their imagination, they can meet their students on their level and readily invent or promote games to make learning fun. (Fazzi & Petersmeyer, 2001, suggest many additional games and fun activities to teach O&M skills and concepts.) Children also invent or introduce their own games that can be recruited into the service of learning O&M.

Children are responsive to personifications and play acting. For example, naming landmarks, infusing them with personalities, and having them talk to the student has definite appeal. Or if going down a steep hill is fun, but the return trip has little appeal, students can become *The Little Engine That Could*, and they will chug enthusiastically up an "I-think-I-can hill," possibly taxing their teacher. Students also enjoy hare and tortoise races, which can be used to encourage those who tend to dawdle to increase their speed. Timers and stopwatches can also be used to create the excitement of a "race" even when the student is only competing against the clock or his or her previous record.

Students can become detectives, solving mysteries and using environmental clues and landmarks to detect their way through an adventure, when in reality the adventure may be as mundane as traveling to the school office. Treasure hunts can be created with large-print or braille clues at each succeeding landmark.

Students can make "cane music" by employing their canes as percussive tools to beat out rhythms on a variety of objects or to drag them across textured or variegated surfaces. A cane can extract an endless array of sounds and rhythms from such items as metal poles, garbage cans, wooden fences, metal gratings, guy-wire covers, wooden doors,

Students are motivated to learn when they are having fun. Important O&M skills can be taught in the course of everyday activities, such as a trip to McDonald's, where students learn bus travel, eating, and money management skills (their money is in the white envelopes they are receiving).

landscaping stones, gravel, dried leaves, bushes, and so forth. It is possible to have lessons whose supposed objective is the recording of the student's "cane music." One student took his "cane music" home and sound mixed it with other sounds, including barking dogs and music, to create his own composition.

Tape recorders can be used in a variety of ways. When used to tape an entire lesson, they bring a bigger-than-life quality to bear upon the lesson. Every sound within the time frame of the lesson is immutably preserved. This is dramatic and impressive. Students will replay the tapes, sometimes over and over (perhaps to the consternation of their parents) and thereby relive the experience, complete with the instruction of their O&M specialist. What could be better?

Extrinsic Rewards

Sometimes neither the fun of a creative lesson nor the intrinsic incentive of learning new and useful skills is sufficient to motivate a student. In these instances, the O&M specialist can try to find a special reward to offer in return for completed lessons. For example, listening to music

This student on a community mobility trip was highly motivated by the chance to buy a Mother's Day gift with his own money.

can be used to reward a reluctant student when he or she is allowed to take listening breaks or to have a period of music time at the end of the lesson. One young blind student worked harder when he could look forward to riding a tricycle in hot pursuit of a beeping goal locator after each lesson.

Token economies, involving point charts and prizes, can also be used to encourage a student to perform. Students who perform learning tasks willingly and accurately may be awarded points or actual tokens that they can accumulate and exchange for a prize or special privilege. The student or teacher may record the points on a tactile or large-print chart. The American Printing House for the Blind features a tactile and audible point chart (see the Resources section). It makes a sound when each point button is pressed, which some students enjoy.

Such extrinsic motivators have definite value when used appropriately. However, all avenues that challenge a student's desire to learn and tap intrinsic motivation should be explored so that they will not become dependent on external "payoffs."

OVERCOMING OBSTACLES

Despite the importance of achieving O&M skills for the independence of students who are visually impaired, learning cannot take place unless students want to learn. Students do not always come to O&M motivated to learn, and their degrees of motivation may fluctuate, reflecting the various states of their lives and health. In addition to making lessons as interesting and fun as possible to help students become involved in learning, it is also important for the O&M specialist to be sensitive to the circumstances that negatively affect motivation and to counteract them in ways that engender a desire to learn.

Self-Esteem versus Overprotection

The process of building motivation cannot be addressed without talking about self-esteem and some things that can erode it. Some children may become reluctant to try new or difficult things if they have had repeated failures. Although children who are blind or visually impaired often experience great successes, at times some of them experience failure because they did not receive the opportunities and support to succeed in new or difficult experiences. Their self-esteem can suffer as a result of becoming objects of overprotection from anxious and well-intentioned children and adults. If other people see them as helpless and vulnerable and rush to their assistance to shield them from a "threatening" world, it contributes to a sense of inadequacy. Conversely, if the O&M specialist can demonstrate their ability to function on their own, it can build students' self-esteem and confidence and stimulate greater willingness in others to encourage and support increased independence.

Webster's defines *overprotect* as "to protect or shield unduly or excessively." For the purposes of this discussion, I would like to extend the definition to include "to do for others what they can do for themselves." A fine line divides appropriate protectiveness from overprotection, and no member of a visually impaired student's support network is exempt from becoming overprotective. For many parents of children who are visually impaired or blind, as well as many workers in the helping professions, helping children can insidiously supercede helping them to help themselves, as was the case with Lavonne:

> Lavonne, a second-grade student who is blind and has mild cerebral palsy who had moved from another school district, resisted getting off the bus at school in the mornings and balked when instructed to travel independently, even for short distances. He frequently cried and threw his long cane away, with the result that the special day class instructional aide would then take him using the human guide technique.
>
> Lavonne's O&M specialist arranged a home visit with Lavonne's grandmother, who was the primary caregiver, to discuss Lavonne's behavior. In response to the O&M specialist's questions regarding Lavonne's independence at home, his grandmother revealed that family members guided him almost everywhere outside the house, including to his swing set in the backyard and to and from the bus in the mornings and afternoons. When he was inside the house they also guided him from room to room. When asked why they did so, his grandmother explained that they did not want him to get hurt, scared, or lost. She stated that the backyard had bumps and holes in it, and she was afraid Lavonne would fall. Inside he might run into the walls or trip on toys in the hall. The route to and from the curb where the bus stopped was dangerous because of a hose that snaked across the sidewalk. Also, to get to the sidewalk, Lavonne would need to travel on the driveway, in which a large, inoperative truck cab was parked.
>
> The O&M specialist agreed that there were potential hazards in Lavonne's environment but asked the grandmother to let her conduct O&M lessons with Lavonne at home. The grandmother reluctantly agreed and joined the lessons as an observer where she watched Lavonne safely grow in skills and independence. Lavonne learned to travel within the house from room to room and to the front and back exits. He learned to locate his swings and to use them independently. He also learned to travel the route to his bus stop, which involved negotiating the unpredictable hose and walking by the huge truck cab.
>
> Initially, the grandmother and the rest of the family, as well as Lavonne, had difficulty accepting that Lavonne could learn to be more independent. They felt a heightened sense of responsibility toward Lavonne that had grown from their perception that his disabilities kept him from independent, safe travel.

Lavonne had accepted their perception that the world was dangerous and inaccessible to him and learned to use negative behavior to get people outside the family to "take care" of him so he would not have to get hurt, scared, or lost. Learning to travel independently at home helped Lavonne to gain a more confident perspective regarding his learning to travel independently at school. It also permitted his family members to modify their perceptions of his vulnerability to harm in an environment that they regarded as benign for themselves.

When children are prohibited from acting and from the consequences of their actions, or when they are prevented from interacting independently with their environment and those who populate it, they will not be able to learn from experience—by making mistakes and correcting them and thereby achieving a sense of accomplishment and confidence. Overprotection may cause them to become passive and manipulative. Studies have revealed that when people are given more responsibility, they take more initiative and are more confident and independent as a result (Langer, 1989).

Working Yourself Out of a Job

Helping students to become more confident and independent is a main goal of O&M instruction. O&M specialists are in a prime position to educate others about overprotection, but they also must be vigilant lest they fall prey to it themselves. Maintaining the philosophy of "working oneself out of a job" and adopting the perspective that "doing less is more" counteract the tendency to overprotect. In other words, O&M specialists need to remember that the aim of O&M instruction is not to *help* students to travel, but to enable them to travel safely by themselves. Achieving this goal sometimes entails stepping back and *not* helping the students, so they can help themselves. Once that goal is accomplished, the specialists' task is done.

To work yourself out of a job involves continually pulling back and redefining goals, as well as pulling yourself free from the web of dependence that students appealingly, and often invisibly, weave. The mere appearance of "blindness," regardless of ability, frequently invokes a helping response in people with sight. A student who is visually impaired or blind may look or act in a helpless manner, but, nonetheless, be able to accomplish a task in his or her own time and way. Often it is necessary for a teacher to run interference, fending off well-intentioned helpers just to ensure that students have the freedom to travel to the bathroom or cafeteria or through the supermarket checkout stand independently. Otherwise, children may grow up so overhelped that they have no confidence in their ability to do things for or by themselves.

The concept of working yourself out of a job applies to other important people in the students' lives, as well as to the O&M specialist. It is essential to communicate to them that when they adopt the long view, doing less to help their children is ultimately doing more. At first, this approach may be strongly resisted, especially by people who habitually have done things differently. Students will resist. Parents, teachers, aides, and the sighted public will resist and will attempt to intervene when they see students who are visually impaired or blind forging their unique paths to independence. For people who have been custodial aides for several years, who are used to maximum involvement in caring for the most intimate needs of students, dropping back to take a hands-off position may feel wrong and be threatening to their self-concept.

Overprotection stems from a variety of motivations. Sometimes the need to be needed prompts people to do too much. Sometimes it is just easier (and faster) to do a task themselves. Regardless of the motive, overprotection needs to be counteracted in a constructive manner. To facilitate the introduction of the new "less-is-more" perspective, it is helpful to invite such important others to observe lessons so that they can see firsthand what the students are capable of doing, as was done with Anita's mother:

> The mother of Anita, an 8 year old who is blind, burst into tears when she first saw her child walking independently down the middle of a school hall using a long cane. "I had no idea she could do that," she exclaimed. Until then, Anita's family had used the human guide technique to take Anita everywhere, even from the living room to her bedroom.

Another effective strategy is to videotape the student performing independently. This tape may then be shared with other school personnel and sent home to the parents. Working in the home and home neighborhood with the parents present is also helpful.

Often people are unaware of the birthright of rich potential awaiting their children who are blind or visually impaired. Introducing parents to independent students and adults who are blind or visually impaired can also be helpful in creating images of potential ability that they can transfer to their own children.

When teachers choose to confront overprotectiveness, they move into a position of influence from which they can encourage the development of new attitudes that free the important others and the children with whom they work. People can learn supportive ways to usher students into fulfilling their maximum potential, rather than doing things for them. Through interactions with other team members—inservice training and education, monitoring the students at home and in school, and consultation—teachers can introduce strategies that enable rather than curtail students' independence. (For a further discussion, see the section on the support team in Chapter 9.) Team members can be taught to step back and help the children learn to do for themselves and to experience independence. Once students have a taste of independence, they will not want to relinquish it.

Emphasizing Ability

When the O&M specialist encounters overprotected students whose self-image is founded on a sense of helplessness and whose intrinsic motivation and creative thinking skills have become depressed as a consequence, the challenge is to counteract low self-esteem and nurture the regrowth of the students' self-concept by emphasizing ability. The children can learn to feel competent and independent and capable, regardless of their disability and in spite of their history of help from others, just as Lavonne did.

For O&M specialists to facilitate their students' ability, it is necessary to acknowledge and discard the ideal of normalcy that may hover like a spectral icon, both in their minds and in the minds of others. Ability for students with disabilities is going to look different from the norm. Adaptations may be necessary. Students may use assistive devices, may take more time, and may travel along different routes that are safer for them. They may communicate by means other than speech. Students who are visually impaired can learn to take pride in performing to the best of their own abilities.

Students also need to learn to feel competent and independent in their own estimation. A strong self-image is based on their sense of what *they* can do, not on the teacher's approval of what they can do. Praise can strengthen students' self-concept when it emphasizes ability, rather than reflects value judgments or "ratings." For example, when a student crosses a busy four-lane street independently and safely for the first time, instead of simply saying, "You did a great job!" it is actually more supportive to say, "You crossed the street safely and independently" or "I like how you crossed the street safely and independently." The shift from making a value judgment to emphasizing ability places the responsibility for students' actions on the students and enables them to "own" their ability. Asking students to express how they feel about their performance similarly encourages them to view themselves as autonomous individuals.

When a student is close to mastery and accomplishes a task independently for the first time, but with a flaw, it may be more supportive to accept the performance as fulfilling the assignment, letting the student feel the strength of his or her success. The flaw can be worked out on the next trial, as in the following example:

> Christine, a student with low vision, cerebral palsy, and developmental delays, made a purchase at the checkout stand independently for the first time but failed to thank the clerk with enough volume to be heard. The teacher said,"You traveled through the line and bought the bananas all by yourself. I like how you put the change and the receipt in your fanny pack and said 'thank you.' I wonder if the clerk was able to hear you?" The teacher knew that projecting her voice to say "thank you" with sufficient loudness could be practiced in a role-playing situation and emphasized as a primary goal the next time Christine made a purchase.

Accepting a task that was accomplished independently, in spite of a flaw, is especially important when working with young children and children with severe disabilities. This is not to say that interventions for safety's sake should be suspended. Handling corrective interventions with sensitivity can go a long way toward nurturing self-esteem. Using phrases such as "You need to," "must," or "should" do thus and such puts the student under the compulsion of the teacher's authority. However, saying, "See if you can find the exit," "What can you do to make yourself more safe?" or ". . . to solve this problem?" respects the student's autonomy and emphasizes ability.

When students develop a sense of their own ability, they will project an "I want to do it myself" attitude, as Timothy did:

After being pushed everywhere by his parents or an aide, Timothy, a passive and dependent young boy who is blind and has quadriplegia, learned to use a one-armed wheelchair to go from the front door of the school to his classroom by trailing walls with his curb detectors and by using auditory clues and object perception. It took him a year to learn to do so accurately on a consistent basis. He owned the accomplishment, and his self-concept expanded to include a desire for independent mobility. One day, a substitute aide who did not know Timothy assumed that he was dependent for mobility on the route to class and started to push him. Timothy loudly proclaimed, "I can do it by myself." Startled by his assertiveness, the aide dropped back and then witnessed that he could, indeed, do it by himself.

Once students have begun to develop their mobility skills, it is important to nurture their independence.

A student can learn to refuse assistance that is intrusive and unsuitable.

Another way to nurture self-esteem and encourage ability is to solicit a student's input in the IEP and lesson planning and evaluative processes. What are the student's goals for mobility? How does the student see the O&M lessons as serving his or her needs? How does the student view his or her mobility performance on various tasks? When the student's ideas and opinions are acknowledged and respected, he or she is affirmed as the subject of a learning process, rather than the object of a teaching process.

Some students will grow in self-esteem as they learn to talk about their O&M abilities with others. Students can be the stars of training sessions that demonstrate mobility devices and techniques to other students or members of the school staff. They can introduce their canes and teach rudimentary cane and human guide techniques to their peers. Doing so will fascinate their peers with sight and bolster the confidence of the visually impaired students as they are recognized as authorities on their unique travel abilities.

Role Models and Role Modeling

When students can meet and interact with older role models who are visually impaired or blind, their self-concepts can expand through identification with people who have similar disabilities. They benefit from having living examples of people who have had similar experiences. An older visually impaired or blind person can be invited to talk to the visually impaired student and his or her class, and the students can be encouraged to prepare and ask questions.

> In the West Contra Costa Unified School District, the program for students with visual impairments hosted a series of potluck evenings with Nick, a professional in adaptive computer technology who is blind. The students in the program and their families and teachers attended. Nick told his story and shared his feelings about growing up with a disability; about his many struggles; about what he might have done differently, given hindsight; and about ways of coping successfully to have a satisfying, productive life. Everyone fell in love with him, hanging on his words and asking countless questions.

Making role models accessible to students and their families can go a long way to counteract their isolation and sense of being different.

Fear as an Impediment to Motivation

Fear is a common emotion experienced by all people. It is not unusual to find that students have fears that constrict their curiosity and prevent them from exploring the world with full freedom and interest. Fear can also depress motivation to a disabling degree. Some students who are visually impaired or blind may have histories of multiple hospitalizations, surgeries, or physical, verbal, or sexual abuse. Fear is a common outgrowth of such experiences and can be a difficult companion on mobility lessons. It can color students' attitudes toward becoming independent, having new experiences, and using adaptive aids. Students may fear that they will be abandoned if they are left alone, even for a moment, in a parked car or if they cannot hear the teacher's presence. They may be afraid of dogs, which can be a real problem when traveling in the local neighborhood, where every other garage or yard has a barking dog. They may fear traveling on escalators or soliciting aid in the supermarket. Students may resist using a long cane or monocular because they see them as advertisements of vulnerability that invite abuse, either physical or emotional.

Fear, as defined by Webster's, is "an unpleasant emotional state characterized by anticipation of pain or great distress and accompanied by heightened autonomic activity, especially involving the nervous system." Fear may not be based in a student's present experience, but projects an imagined threatening outcome into the future. Because of the anticipatory element of fear, it is difficult to counteract.

Fears may be real or irrational and may be deeply ingrained habitual responses. Periodically, the O&M specialist must deal with the effects of fear on students' mobility performance. Sometimes students outgrow their fears naturally as they mature and increase in experience and confidence. In other instances, deliberate intervention strategies are necessary. It may be possible to desensitize a student to a feared object by repeated exposure to it in a nonthreatening manner, as was done with George:

> George had a continual fear of dogs, although he had never had a bad experience with a dog. He said he was afraid of dogs because his mother was. Mobility lessons were designed with dogs as a major focus. Dog breeds and habits were discussed at length. Humorous impersonations were acted out, with the

teacher and George becoming talking dogs. George and the teacher visited two local dogs, befriending their owner and learning the dogs' names and habits. George's favorite mobility goal became traveling into the community to visit the dogs. His fear was replaced by fascination, and his travel through the community became freer as a result.

The fear of being stigmatized by using mobility and optical aids, such as the long cane or monocular, is difficult to counteract, especially among teenagers who highly esteem the acceptance of their peers and fear that appearing different will cause them to be ridiculed and rejected or abused. Students with such fears, nonetheless, may consent to learn to use a monocular to view distant objects and a long cane for safer travel and identification purposes if they are given lessons in an area where they are sure that they will not run into their peers. This does not mean that they will necessarily continue to use their aids after training is complete. Some students will prefer to use their feet to explore the terrain tactilely and even to risk falling down unanticipated stairs in the process. They may also prefer to wander until, if lucky, they happen upon their destination, rather than resort to using a monocular to read a street sign. Their training must not be regarded as an exercise in futility, but as the laying of a foundation of skills they may fall back on in times of need or when their attitudes change, as occurred with Scott:

> Scott, a student with deteriorating vision and night blindness who never used his cane outside of lessons and proclaimed to other students who were visually impaired that he hated his cane, reported proudly that he had used it to travel independently to the neighborhood store after dark one night. Before that time, he had depended solely on his brother to be his human guide at night. This was an important and courageous first step toward greater independence. He learned that he could travel without his brother at night if he used his cane.

Teachers need to take the time to get to know their students. This enables them to discover the obstacles to learning that a particular student may need to overcome, as well as how to foster the student's self-esteem and desire to learn. Building motivation does not happen all at once, but is a gradual process, enabling students to enjoy creative, fun lessons and take pride in their growing skills and abilities.

PROMOTING SAFETY

For O&M specialists and teachers, safety is a constant focus and a primary consideration underlying everything they do. Safety is an essential part of every lesson. O&M specialists teach survival skills in the most basic sense. Their students rely on them to teach practices that will promote safe travel for a lifetime to come. O&M specialists are also responsible for their students, not only when the students are with them, but also as consultants providing informed recommendations to other educational team members about the students' overall safety as travelers who are blind or visually impaired. It is important that O&M specialists approach their task as promoting the attainment of goals methodically and safely in a potentially life- or health-threatening environment.

This section discusses some general safety guidelines. Additional safety considerations are discussed in Chapter 6, The Domains: Home, School, and Community and the sections Students in Wheelchairs in Chapter 8 and Legal and Safety Issues in Chapter 9.

Emergency Preparedness

It is critical to carry basic and emergency information about all your students at all times in case of a medical emergency or other unexpected situation. This information includes the students' addresses and telephone numbers; names and telephone numbers of important others; medical information; and emergency procedures for individual students, especially those who are medically fragile or have diabetes, asthma, or epilepsy. You should also carry a copy of the school district's particular emergency policies and procedures and important telephone numbers at each school. It is also a good idea to carry permission forms signed by the students' parents or guardians to allow you to obtain emergency medical treatment in case a student requires medical procedures. Having all this information on hand can save time and eliminate confusion and other barriers to prompt action in an emergency. Students should be taught to carry and present their own emergency information, if necessary. You should also carry a small first-aid kit (including rubber gloves) at all times, in case there are minor injuries or mishaps, and be prepared to observe universal precautions.

Vehicle Safety

When transporting a young child in a car, it is important to comply with safety laws regarding the use of infant seats and air bags. You may bring a scale to school or use the one in the nurse's office to weigh the student to determine if he or she should be transported in an infant seat or positioned to avoid injury from an air bag that cannot be disabled. If a student weighs less than the legally mandated weight, he or she must be secured in an infant seat. If it is necessary to transport children in a personal car, it is also crucial to pay careful attention to the safety of the car and the proper insurance coverage (see the section on Legal and Safety Issues in Chapter 9).

Weatherproofing

The weather that accompanies different seasons of the year is a major aspect of the setting in which O&M instruction takes place, since so much of the teaching environment is the outdoors. Weather is, by its very nature, unpredictable. It thus behooves the O&M specialist to be prepared. It is helpful to stay on top of weather reports, however fickle, and to adopt a long view of weather potentials. Students need to learn to travel safely and comfortably in all types of weather, so a change in the weather should not be a reason to cancel lessons. In the event of drastic extremes of inclement weather, however, it is helpful to have alternative lesson plans available.

Protecting Against the Sun

With the destruction of the ozone layer, traveling outdoors can be an occupational hazard for the O&M specialist who may spend many hours a week in the sun, as well as for students, especially those with albinism. Several approaches may be used to shield bodies from the harmful rays of the sun. *Sunscreens* may be applied to all exposed areas of the skin. When buying a sunscreen be sure that it is SPF 15 or higher and provides full-spectrum protection. Parents should be consulted regarding the use of sunscreens and be encouraged to buy them for their children. Because of the possibility of allergic reactions, it is best that students have their own pretested sunscreens and know how to apply them. Another approach is to wear clothing that thoroughly covers the body and provides adequate SPF protection. (For one source of sun-safe clothing and related products see the Resources section.)

Additional gear includes various hats and visors. Most students are willing to wear visors and some especially enjoy hats with sports teams' logos. Students who are photosensitive benefit from various types of dark glasses, including photo gray, clip-on, absorbent, or other wraparound varieties (see the Resources section), or regular dark glasses. All should provide adequate UV protection. Some students, although photosensitive, experience significantly diminished vision if they wear dark glasses, but they may respond well to wearing visors to shade their eyes.

Inclement Weather

Staying warm and staying dry are two primary considerations when traveling in inclement weather. Warm clothes are a fairly universal solution to cold weather. If a student arrives underdressed, however, the classroom teacher may have an extra jacket that the student can use, or it may be possible to borrow a jacket from the school's lost and found.

A cane traveler may experience particular discomfort in cold weather because of the exposed cane hand. It is important to retain the sensitivity of uncovered fingers to receive tactile input with the greatest clarity. Sensitivity can be retained if a student wears a specially designed cane glove or gloves that do not cover the full length of the fingers. Such gloves may be purchased or devised by cutting off the fingers of regular gloves. It is helpful if the teacher has a pair of universal-sized gloves with finger tips cut off for students who come unprepared. Students who do not use canes may benefit from wearing gloves or mittens or putting their hands in their pockets.

To stay dry, students should be encouraged to use their own rain gear, including raincoats, hats, umbrellas, and boots or waterproof shoes. Since students sometimes come unprepared, it is a good idea to have an extra umbrella, poncho, and rainproof headgear stored in the trunk of the car.

One of the most useful items of clothing an O&M specialist can have is a pair of comfortable rubber boots or waterproof or rubber shoes that will keep his or her feet dry when traveling in rainy weather or over wet terrain. The O&M specialist who works in the public schools frequently walks through parking lots at schools and in the community, most of which turn into lakes during rainy weather, or on wet grass and sand in public parks. It does not hurt to carry rubber footwear in one's car for such eventualities.

Cutting the finger tips off a pair of inexpensive gloves can minimize the discomfort of cold weather while preserving tactile sensitivity for a cane traveler. This light-sensitive student also wears dark amber glasses.

Wheelchairs and Inclement Weather

Students in wheelchairs have unique needs relative to travel in inclement weather. In cold weather, they may have difficulty operating the controllers of their power chairs. A remedy may be gloves or mittens. Mittens may be necessary if paralysis of the hands makes it difficult or impossible to apply gloves, but mittens may reduce fine motor control. On rainy days, students may wear ponchos that cover their whole wheelchairs or use clip-on umbrellas that attach to the wheelchairs. When traveling in rainy weather, it is advisable to avoid going through deep puddles, which would get the batteries of power chairs wet.

Rain

Rainy weather can be an ally in the teaching and learning process. The diverse sounds of the rain as it falls on the surrounding surfaces provide the sensible medium by which a person who is blind may experience the continuity of a three-dimensional landscape, which is otherwise accessible only by sight. In his book, *Touching the Rock: An Experience of Blindness*, Hull (1990) described in striking fashion the auditory experience of three-dimensional space:

> Rain has a way of bringing out the contours of everything; it throws a colored blanket over previously invisible things; instead of an intermittent and thus fragmented world, the steadily falling rain creates continuity of acoustic experience.
>
> I hear the rain pattering on the roof above me, dripping down the walls to my left and right, splashing from the drain pipe at ground level on my left, while further over to the left there is a lighter patch as the rain falls almost inaudibly upon a large leafy shrub. On the right, it is drumming with a deeper, steadier sound, upon the lawn. I can even make out the contour of the lawn which rises to the right in a little hill. The sound of the rain is different and shapes out the curvature for me. Still further to the right, I hear the rain sounding upon the fence which divides our property from the next door. In front, the contours of the path and the steps are marked out, right down to the garden gate. Here the rain is striking the concrete, here it is splashing into the shallow pools which have already formed. . . . . Further out the sounds are less detailed. I can hear the rain falling on the road, and the swish of the cars as they pass up and down. . . . *The rain presents the fullness of an entire situation all at once, not merely remembered, not in anticipation, but actually and now. The rain gives a sense of perspective and of the actual relationships of one part of the world to another."* [Italics added]

For students, rain can provide a similar experience. Traffic patterns become accessible in a new way as vehicles swish by. Rolling down the windows of the car while driving similarly makes cars approaching and passing in the opposite lanes increasingly palpable. Going outdoors on a rainy day is an opportunity for exploring the shapes of outdoor objects and space auditorily, thereby expanding students' perceptions of the world.

Determining Appropriate Goals

In setting O&M goals and designing lessons for students, the O&M specialist has to take into consideration whether the student is capable of performing particular skills in a safe manner. Often the O&M specialist will have a strong sense of his or her students' abilities and weaknesses based on assessment results, but it can help to have an informed second opinion from another O&M specialist. This is especially true in situations when other team members have inflated or unduly low estimations of a student's ability to perform certain activities safely.

Some students cannot learn safety precautions because of such factors as age, level of functioning, or lack of vision (see, for example, the discussion of street crossings in Chapter 6). In such cases, safety may need to be ensured through proper monitoring and environmental adaptations. There are certain situations, such as the following, in which school personnel simply are not able to ensure a student's safety:

> Two members of the educational team approached an O&M specialist to request that she provide O&M training for Larry, a high school student with low vision and severe cognitive deficits. The teachers were justifiably concerned when they discovered that the student was allowed to roam his neighborhood after school under the "supervision" of neighborhood children. He frequently crossed the street with no regard to approaching traffic.
>
> During the O&M specialist's assessment of the situation, her review of the student's psychological records and consultation with the school psychologist revealed that the student had no concept of cause-and-effect relationships and hence the danger imposed by approaching vehicles. Because of her experience working with him and his cognitive level, the psychologist concluded that Larry would never develop these skills. Consequently, the O&M specialist wrote a report quoting the psychologist and recommending closer parental monitoring, rather than training Larry in street-crossing skills. Failing that, it would be necessary to notify Child Protective Services that there was negligence resulting in child endangerment. The input from the psychologist helped to give credibility to the O&M specialist's recommendations and to clarify issues of the school's responsibility in the situation.

In such situations, O&M specialists need to be aware of liability issues, as discussed in Chapter 9.

Teaching Safe Attitudes

O&M specialists can ensure that their students are safe during lessons through attentive monitoring and appropriate instructional interventions. I have no shame about sharing aphorisms with my students. It *is* better to be safe than sorry and haste *does* makes waste. I also share stories about people who have had accidents because of unsafe practices. Students can be convinced of the importance of a "safety-first" attitude. They can also be taught to identify "I need help" situations and to solicit aid appropriately. Students also need to learn to wait and to see time as their ally in situations that require critical decision making, such as those involved in crossing streets. When students gain solid skills in a methodical and cumulative manner, they will naturally grow in confidence. This, too, makes them safer.

Teaching safe travel strategies to students goes beyond the basic logistics of O&M practice and encompasses strategies that promote safety in general. Students should be taught a commonsense approach to dealing with strangers, night travel, and travel in questionable neighborhoods. They should be taught to travel in pairs in risky situations or to forgo travel until they can do it safely. They should be taught to carry money in ways that will not attract theft. They need to learn to use the phone and to dial 911 in designated situations.

Finally, O&M specialists need to function as safety role models. Their example can make a strong and lasting impression on students. O&M specialists may take shortcuts and adopt some questionable practices when traveling on their own, but when they are with students, they should model only the most conservative practices.

This chapter has focused on promoting approaches and conditions that facilitate learning O&M skills and techniques. Chapter 6 examines more closely the primary environments in which O&M is taught—the home, the school, and the community—and the issues that tend to arise in each area.

6

The Domains: Home, School, and Community

As students grow, mature, and develop their orientation and mobility (O&M) skills, their travel experiences will change accordingly by expanding through the ever-widening spheres of home, school, community, and extended community. It is the job of the O&M specialist to facilitate a student's growth, helping to develop age- and ability-appropriate skills, nurturing confidence, and counteracting overprotection in each of these domains. Ongoing observation and assessment of the individual student's abilities and needs will help the O&M specialist determine what skills to address and within which domains. The different domains each present unique challenges that highlight skills that need to be learned. Although a student tends to travel in increasingly greater and more challenging environments as time passes, he or she may also need to continue to work in each of the domains to master increasingly complex skills that are required there.

HOME

Students' homes are their domains of origin, the places where they have their earliest learning experiences. The O&M specialist plays an important role in supporting students' growth in this setting. Home visits are an integral part of serving students, especially if the students are preschoolers or are new to the program. It is important to examine a student's home and yard, if there is one, and to determine how he or she is functioning within this environment. The O&M specialist should schedule home visits to meet with the parent or primary caregiver, to observe the student, and to instruct the student and parent in strategies to make the student safer and more independent at home. The home is a good environment in which to work on basic skills and to instruct the parent in the support of basic skills.

Home visits can be revealing in that they provide opportunities to observe the day-to-day modus operandi of the parents and child. Do the family members wait on the child hand and foot? Does the child have chores and responsibilities? How well is the child oriented to his or her home environment? Parents and other family members may readily share concerns regarding the child's current travel and potential for future independent travel. The O&M specialist can troubleshoot and brainstorm with them to isolate areas for growth.

Issues of overprotection, discussed in detail in Chapter 5, are especially apparent in the home. It is important to approach them in a frank manner, supporting and encouraging the parents by conducting lessons in the home so that they can witness their child's abilities in more independent mobility, as in the following example:

> On one home visit, an O&M specialist discovered that when Sally entered the front door, her well-meaning parents whisked away her cane, folded it, and stored it on the top shelf of the hall closet where she could not reach it. Students with good spatial skills may not need their canes within a consistent, safe, familiar environment and travel competently using object perception, trailing, and protective arm techniques. However, Sally had difficulty with spatial skills and became easily disoriented, even within this familiar environment. Her parents had resorted to taking her around the house using human guide techniques. Sally became a more competent traveler when permitted to retain and manage her cane. For Sally, using a cane was more effective than using basic skills because it enabled her to search her environment with maximum efficiency prior to moving.

An important home route for a student to learn is the one from his or her house to the school bus and back. Sometimes obstacles are present on this route that impede the student's independence, such as a long flight of stairs from the house to the walk or an iron gate that is difficult to open. Rather than view these objects as obstacles to independence, the O&M specialist can see them as opportunities for growth when they are drawn into the compass of an O&M lesson and the student is taught ways to negotiate them—as Lavonne, mentioned in Chapter 5, learned to negotiate the hose and truck in his driveway.

SCHOOL

The ongoing goal for students is to take care of their basic needs in an increasingly independent, although possibly adapted, manner. The school offers continuing challenges to this end. With the appropriate support to students, the school can be an environment that compels progressive growth in independence. At first, a student will be challenged by learning his or her way around the classroom. Once this home base is established, more far-reaching travel opportunities can be explored. Important routes to learn include these:

1. the round trip from the bus to the classroom.

2. the round trip from the classroom to the bathroom, including negotiating bathroom stalls, urinals, and sinks, and the logistics of cane storage in this environment. (This process may be facilitated by a same-sex aide when necessary.)

3. the round trip from the classroom to the cafeteria, including negotiating lines, gathering food, and locating a table.

4. the round trip from the classroom to the playground and equipment.

5. the round trip from the classroom to the school office.

6. the round trip from a resource room to mainstream classes and electives or other specialized classes.

7. the routes from classroom to classroom for mainstreamed students in secondary schools.

A particular challenge to many students is traveling in crowds during passing periods. The churning mass of bodies and the heightened sound level obscures environmental clues and architectural details. Some students may be at a total loss in this type of situation. Several approaches to this challenge may be used. Regardless of their degrees of vision and independent traveling abilities, it may be most effective for students to walk close to the wall and to trail it visually or by hand or cane. A wall provides a constant in an environment that is

Students need to learn a number of routes at school, including the route from the school bus to their classroom.

changing. By trailing, students will be sure to locate intersections and will not be swept through them when they need to make a turn. If students are distracted in crowds, it may be better to adjust their schedules slightly so that they leave class a little early to travel when the coast is still clear. Another solution is for them to solicit assistance in the form of a human guide or traveling companion.

Teachers of students with visual impairments who work with preschoolers and elementary-aged students in a self-contained class are often confronted with the task of moving their entire class from one place to another for special events or fire drills. Getting students to travel in a line can be a daunting project when they tend to travel at different rates of speed and have a whole range of visual anomalies, cognitive abilities, and behavioral styles. It is possible to teach them to hold onto a rope at designated positions and to travel single file following a role model at the head of the line. To identify their unique positions in the line and to promote spacing and retention of grasp, large wooden beads in a variety of shapes, colors, and textures (such as those available in the bead-stringing kit available from the American Printing House for the Blind) can be affixed to rope or heavy twine at intervals. A shape and/or texture or color may be permanently assigned to each child. Initially, the children have to be closely monitored by the teacher and aides to retain their grasp and spacing, but in time they will learn to walk in line.

When teaching classroom aides or paraeducators who will supervise supported travel around the school, it is essential to emphasize the importance of limiting verbal interactions to prompting so as to minimize distractions to the students. Many students and their aides want to socialize when traveling. However, most students have difficulty focusing on travel, retaining orientation, and exercising object perception if their attention is otherwise engaged. The aide should travel at an appropriate distance, adopting an "invisible presence," unless he or she is needed to prompt by giving a physical or verbal cue to the student to correct or reinforce a behavior. To satisfy social needs, talking breaks may be structured into the day or held briefly at the end of the route if it is convenient.

The attention of the O&M specialist may be required for such special events as dance, music, and drama productions, to help figure out routes and the logistics of travel in an undefined space, such as a stage. In situations such as these, students can measure distances they have to travel by counting steps, and visual and tactile markers can be created using fluorescent and textured nonskid tapes to denote distinct positions and create lines of travel. Sometimes human guide assistance can be choreographed into the production.

COMMUNITY

The community has a potent attraction to students of all ages. The allure of such activities as exploring one's neighborhood, going shopping, and experiencing recreational and work opportunities is a powerful motivation for students to learn independent travel skills. This section examines several of the most significant areas in the domain of the community: becoming acquainted with automobiles, shopping, street crossings, and public transportation.

Vehicle Travel and Familiarization

The automobile is a key link to the extended community and its myriad attractions, especially for preschoolers and elementary-aged students who are too young to learn to travel independently by public transportation. Students, both those with low vision and those who are blind, need to learn, within the scope of their abilities, to find their way around the inside and outside of a car, how to get in and out of it, and how to ride as a passenger. Becoming familiar with cars is an ongoing activity for students who are blind and will not be accomplished in a single exposure. When conducting car-familiarization activities, the O&M specialist needs to take a hands-on approach, encouraging students to explore the whole car tactilely, touching and manipulating its various parts thoroughly—including the tires. Students' hands may get dirty in the process. Moist towelettes are useful for cleaning up afterward, and they can be carried in the glove compartment. Some of the things students need to learn about using a car include the following:

- differentiating the front from the back
- identifying the driver and passenger sides
- differentiating the front door from the back door
- storing the cane against the side of the car to free the hands
- opening *and* locking and closing the door from the outside
- sitting and storing the cane inside
- closing and locking the door from the inside
- fastening and unfastening the seat belt (and why it is used)
- unlocking and opening the door from the inside
- locating and using visors (if a student is light sensitive)
- locating a disabled parking permit and displaying it in the correct location

Mastering these skills may take time, sometimes years. However, it is never too soon to start learning. When these skills are mastered, the student will be an independent passenger.

Students also benefit from having opportunities to explore the interiors of public transit vehicles, such as buses, trains, and rapid transit conveyances. Lessons may be planned in cooperation with the transit companies, which may give students opportunities to "study" stationary vehicles.

On many community lessons, significant amounts of time are often spent driving students to and from the training site, and this time, too, may be used as an opportunity for learning. For example, students can practice memorizing and reciting personal information to the O&M specialist, who can carry a small file with the students' names, parents' names, addresses, telephone numbers, and other important information to keep the facts straight while quizzing the students. The time also may be used to work on generalizing concepts. Students can learn to identify whether the car is going straight, forward, backward, to the right or left, and up or down hills. They can memorize the route to the site and back and direct the specialist by telling him or her the street names and types of turns needed to arrive at the site or to return to school. This is a good way to develop sequencing skills and lays an important foundation for future direction-giving abilities. Car time may also be used to review knowledge related to anticipated or just-completed activities. For example, if the students and O&M specialist are going shopping, they can discuss what the students will buy, to which departments they need to go, whether they need to solicit aid, how much money they have, and so forth.

Supermarket Shopping

Supermarket shopping is often a focal activity for O&M training. Learning the structure and layout of a supermarket is a valuable experience in general O&M. Many travel techniques can be practiced within a supermarket, and sensory perceptions can be refined. The supermarket provides an enormous library of real objects for students to examine minutely. Many students have an impoverished sense of the reality to which people with sight have immediate access. In the supermarket, a student may handle flowers and plants, fruits and vegetables in their whole condition, breads in loaves, packaged meats and fishes, and an endless array of interesting items that, heretofore, may have been merely names without substance. For some it will be a rich vocabulary-building experience as they learn the names and properties of new objects.

Orientation

The approach to teaching shopping depends on a student's visual condition and many other factors that affect ability and performance, such

The supermarket provides an enormous library of real objects for the student to examine minutely.

as age, cognitive function, and the presence of additional impairments. In general, when teaching in a supermarket, it is a good idea to focus first on orientation to the periphery of the store, with the differentiation of sides and front and back in an area-specific manner (as described in the section on orientation in Chapter 7). The student will learn to sequence landmarks and identify different departments by landmark and auditory and olfactory clues (of which there are many). Inner aisles may be accessed by direction taking from landmarks on the periphery and using auditory and olfactory clues for confirmation. Students who are blind will benefit from learning to use the store-provided shopping service whereby they are accompanied by a clerk who locates desired items at their request.

Using Optical Aids

For students with low vision, shopping skills may be enhanced by using monocular telescopes. The students may use this aid to read overhead store directories that identify aisles and the location of specific items. When needed, a magnifier or close-focusing monocular may be used to read prices and information on packages.

Shopping Baskets and Carts

The capable student with a long shopping list can learn to develop a store itinerary to locate specific items. He or she may also learn to use a shopping basket or cart. Students with low vision who use canes may also learn to maneuver a shopping cart. Rudimentary driving lessons are necessary to avoid collisions.

Soliciting Aid

The supermarket is a good place to learn to solicit aid from strangers. Some students are nervous, if not fearful, of this activity and require support and encouragement at first. When a student asks a clerk for directions, such as, "Where is the bakery?" the clerk may respond with a combination of imprecise verbal directions and body language by saying, "Over there" and gesturing vaguely. Students should be taught to explain that they are visually impaired, since it will not necessarily be apparent to a clerk. They should also be taught to repeat back to the clerk what they have heard or interpreted from the clerk's communication. Doing so will show the clerk the degree to which the students have accurately gleaned information from the instructions. The clerk may then refine the directions or give additional help as necessary.

Conducting Transactions

Before they purchase items, students must locate an open checkout stand and, in most cases, travel through a line. Line travel can pose some difficulties to students who are blind because they cannot always detect movement in the line. They can use their canes *gently to* search for and contact the cart or foot of the person in front of them, with the appropriate "Excuse me," of course. Students may be taught to cue into the verbal exchanges of the clerk and customer preceding them to identify their approaching turn. They need to pay particularly close attention to the whole process so they are prepared to present their purchases and have their money ready. At first, students may tend to thrust both money and purchases upon the clerk or present the purchases and neglect to give their money. They need to learn to have their

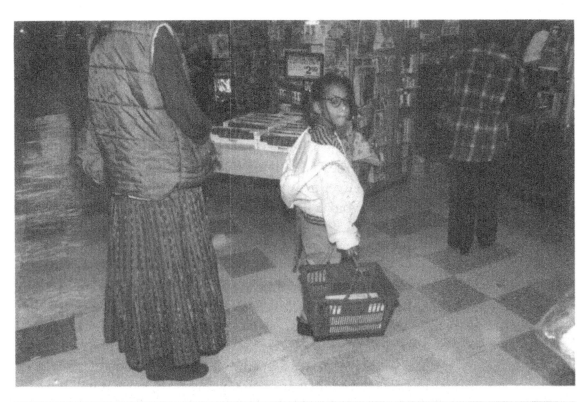

Traveling through a line at a checkout counter and paying for purchases entail a whole host of important skills.

money accessible and to wait for a verbal prompt from the clerk before they extend their money.

Prior to shopping, it bolsters a student's confidence to conduct role-playing activities in which the O&M specialist and student "play store" to solidify the sequence of a transaction and explore a variety of possible dialogues and verbal prompts. The etiquette of a transaction should be explained. Students need to learn to project their voices and to use polite forms, saying "please" and "thank you" at the appropriate junctures in a conversation.

During initial purchasing lessons, the O&M specialist may model the whole procedure and then, step by step, fade into the background, being prepared to prompt, but allowing the student to take on more and more of the responsibility until he or she is fully independent. At first, clerks will direct all of their attention toward the O&M specialist. This tendency may be alleviated with a few words or a gesture directing their attention to the student. Eventually, the clerks will become the primary prompters. With practice and repeated visits, some clerks will even become familiar and skilled members of the team.

It will take more time for most students to conduct a transaction than for the usual customer. This is all right. They are entitled to the time even if there are seven people in line behind them. Students may fumble and drop their change, but this is no cause for panic. It is all a legitimate part of life. Students may grow in their ability to perform independently but may retain a lingering psychological dependence on the O&M specialist, which diminishes their confidence and initiative. At that point, the O&M specialist needs to adopt an "I'm not here" attitude. Students can be encouraged to pretend that the specialist is not with them, and the specialist can withdraw out of their range of vision or ask them to meet him or her at a prearranged rendezvous. The students can be assured that the specialist is not abandoning them and will reappear if they become truly disoriented. Students become more resourceful and creative when the bonds of dependence are loosened and eventually broken.

Money Management

Some students will have already learned or be learning the host of skills related to using money. Money management skills include understanding the respective values of coins and bills; identifying coins visually or tactilely; and keeping bills of different denominations folded in different and consistent ways so that students won't offer a ten-dollar bill when a one-dollar bill is all that is required! Shopping is, of course, an excellent way to teach and reinforce money-management skills.

For some students, especially those with canes, shopping will be facilitated if they use a fanny pack worn in front where they can store their money. Using a wallet is a more complex skill, which can be developed simultaneously if desired. Wallets should be firm and have distinctly separate coin sections. A woman's leather folding wallet with a built in snap-open coin purse works especially well. However, for some students, a fanny pack or pocket will be easier at first.

Another aspect of money management is estimating shopping expenses and comparing them to the amount of money one has to prevent overspending. Students with weak math skills may benefit from learning to use finger math to perform calculations (see Kapperman, Heinze, & Sticken, 2000, pp. 88–89, for an explanation of finger math).

A student can also carry a talking calculator to keep a running account of prices.

Parking Lot Travel

When driving to a site, such as a supermarket in the community, a parking lot poses a unique set of challenges to the traveler. Although traffic moves slowly, more accidents involving pedestrian injuries occur in parking lots than anywhere else. Parking lots are particularly dangerous to ambulatory and wheelchair-using students who are visually impaired, and for students who are blind, they can be nearly impossible to navigate. Most parking lots lack sidewalks, and traffic within them tends to be erratic, so there are no consistent traffic sounds or surges from which to take prompts. If possible, it is a good idea to park in a disabled parking space near the entrance of the place you are going. It may be possible for you to qualify for a disabled parking permit for use when transporting students. This is something that may be worked out in conjunction with the school administration and the Department of Motor Vehicles.

When it is necessary to park in the lot at a distance from the store, there are several strategies to promote safety. Students may stand at the rear of the car to scan. It may be preferable to use the human guide technique with students who are blind. After determining that it is safe to proceed, a student should travel in the middle of the lane facing oncoming traffic to be most visible to drivers who may be pulling out of parking places. It is also a good idea to try to park in areas of the parking lot where there may be sidewalks that lead toward the stores.

Living Skills Unit

Community travel and learning about shopping provide the opportunity for a teacher of visually impaired students who has a group of students to offer a living skills unit. Students can plan, shop, and cook for themselves and others as a class. They may even sell the products of their cooking to raise funds for further shopping and cooking. The class plans menus and develops shopping lists that the various students take with them on their shopping trips. Lists may range from a single item to ambitious quantities of goods, depending on each student's ability to shop.

Street Crossings

Community travel involves learning to move freely in one's neighborhood and within business communities. It also includes learning to use public transportation. To do any of these things independently, a student must learn to cross streets safely. Crossing streets safely is predicated on several abilities, including these:

1. the ability to follow directions

2. comprehension of cause-and-effect relationships

3. a demonstrated understanding of the concept of danger

A student should not be considered a candidate for street-crossing instruction until these abilities have been manifested.

When O&M specialists establish goals for their students, they must bear in mind age- and skill-level appropriateness. Sometimes it is more suitable to consider mental age than chronological age. Mental age is often stated in the summaries of psychological testing that

This student is learning about traffic-pattern concepts by working with a tactile model of the intersection to replicate the structure of the intersection and its traffic patterns.

appear in students' files. It can be illuminating to discuss students with the school psychologist who tested them. This person can give information regarding a student's knowledge of cause-and-effect relationships, ability to sequence, and so forth.

The act of crossing a street brings the student to the apex of a life-and-death situation. It is the most dramatic arena of the learning process in O&M. People get injured and killed crossing streets. For this reason, the task should not be approached lightly. Street-crossing instruction should be structured and sequenced to produce consistent and reliable ability- and age-appropriate skills. It should never be hurried. There is no such thing as a crash course in street crossing. It may take a student years to learn to develop the maturity and skills to cross streets safely, ranging from streets in a quiet residential area to those with complex or freeway-like characteristics. It is beyond the scope of this work to set forth a detailed curriculum for progressing through a course of advancing street-crossing skills. (For a guide to teaching street crossings, see, for example, Guth & Rieser, 1997; Hill & Ponder, 1976.)

Prior to teaching a student street crossing, it is vital to get information about the student's hearing and ability to localize sound, as well as vision, including visual fields. The student who is blind or visually impaired is all the more dependent on hearing. If hearing is impaired or the student is unable to localize sound, when the student has only one functioning ear, or his or her brain lacks a *corpus callosum*, adaptive measures must be taken to refine his or her ability to detect the proximity and location of vehicles. For a student with a restricted visual field or blind spots, methods of eccentric viewing or adaptive scanning should be explored. Students with low vision should be tested in a variety of traffic situations for their ability to detect approaching vehicles by taking them to an intersection commensurate with their level of travel competence and asking them to state when they first perceive vehicles advancing from a variety of directions. This can be an illuminating experience for both the students and the O&M specialist. On a busy or curving street or on a windy day, students may not perceive a vehicle until it is too close to be safe. Some students may perceive the majority of cars at safe distances but will not perceive cars that present low contrast against the street. Given such conditions, the student should ask for help in crossing or identify a safer place to cross.

Public Transportation

As already noted, using public transportation is another aspect of learning to travel around the expanding domain of the community. Because public transportation facilitates access to both the immediate and extended community, learning to use it is exciting, challenging, and anxiety provoking for students who are blind or visually impaired. It is empowering for those who will never drive (see Corn & Rosenblum, 2000, for a complete discussion of transportation for nondrivers with visual impairment). Although a large urban area may encompass a variety of public transit options—including buses, paratransit vehicles, taxis, rapid transit vehicles, and trains—the primary focus of this discussion is on bus travel, since it is common to many different types of areas and the logistics of managing and teaching bus travel can be generalized, to a large extent, to other forms of transportation.

Structuring Lessons

When beginning bus travel instruction with a student, it is important to familiarize the student to the bus. Many students have had prior experience with buses through riding the school bus or city buses with their parents. A field trip for a group of students to a bus company's yard, where they can receive a guided tour of a parked bus, is an excellent way to give them the opportunity to examine a bus closely and experience it in a nonthreatening way.

Students should also be given an overall familiarization lesson on the basic approach to locating the bus stop, catching and boarding the bus; paying the fare; sitting; and riding, stopping, and exiting the bus. This can be accomplished in a brief lesson conducted from one local stop to the next. The familiarization lesson can be undertaken as a round trip by catching the next bus back, or it may be preferable to walk back to the starting point. Actually learning the skills touched on during this overview will be the focus of subsequent lessons.

Once students are oriented to the bus and have some familiarization with bus travel, it is possible to start working on route travel. With youthful and inexperienced students it is best to limit the number of objectives per lesson and to provide maximum support until confidence and ability are developed. Motivation can be built in by tapping students' interests and establishing the relevance of bus travel to the students' experience levels, lives, and needs. For example, students may be motivated to learn to ride a public bus to stop riding the special education bus or to travel to a particular goal such as the mall or regular eye appointments in a neighboring city.

It is also advisable to keep lessons short at first unless the student's motivation is high. It is counterproductive for a student to spend excessive amounts of time standing at a bus stop. This may be a real part of bus travel at times, but it should be avoided in early lessons. It is also important to teach trip planning (as discussed in the following section).

Teaching bus route travel can be divided into the following five stages:

1. *The trip planning level.* Trip planning may take several sessions and will be repeated for each new route. The student will take on more and more responsibility for it as time progresses.

2. *The familiarization level.* The O&M specialist delivers close, active instruction during the whole route. He or she models behavior as necessary and elicits feedback from the student to ensure the absorption of new information.

3. *The maximum support level.* The O&M specialist stays close to the student during the whole route to provide immediate support when necessary and to answer questions. The student is encouraged to act as independently as possible on the basis of knowledge gained from the familiarization level.

4. *The minimum support level.* The O&M specialist sits at the back of the bus or out of the student's visual range. He or she continues to observe the student and is prepared to make active interventions to prompt the student, if necessary. The student is aware of the specialist's proximity but acts independently.

5. *The independent level.* The student catches and rides the bus independently. The O&M specialist follows in a car and meets the student at a prearranged rendezvous.

A number of lessons may be conducted at each level, depending on the needs of the individual student.

Trip Planning

Prior to conducting a lesson on trip planning, the O&M specialist needs to do some homework to ensure the smoothest possible experience for a student, gathering information on bus lines, stops, times, and landmarks. It may not be sufficient simply to phone the transit company once for information. For information about unfamiliar routes, I have found it wise to call three times for the information. If after the third call I have three different trip plans, I reexamine the transit schedule and map and drive the route to verify the accuracy of the information. It is always a good idea to drive the route anyway to become familiar with it, to look for any potential trouble spots, and to identify landmarks. I say this advisedly because of frustrating experiences traveling based on inaccurate information. There may be more than one way to get to a destination. Which one will be best for the student? Once you feel confident about a route, you are prepared to give knowledgeable support to the student.

Students must learn to gather information related to their proposed trips by developing skills in soliciting aid over the telephone and learning to read transit schedules. To be prepared to use information gathered during trip planning, students must have a way to store and organize it. When gathering information by phone, with the permission of the transit information operator, they may record their conversation using a tape recorder and patch cord or similar device attached to the phone. Some telephones with built-in answering machines have the capability of recording conversations directly. If a student records solicited information, he or she may later arrange it into a usable form by entering it on a Trip Planning Information Form like the one illustrated in Figure 6.1. The student may choose to transcribe the information directly from the conversation onto the form while talking on the telephone or to braille it. Direct transcription takes more skill.

When students call for information, they should identify themselves as people who are blind or visually impaired to help obtain more individualized treatment. For accountability and future reference, it is a good idea to ask for and record the operator's name or identification number. If the operator appears to be ill informed, inattentive, or confesses to a lack of knowledge (yes, they sometimes do), the student should ask to speak to a supervisor. This is all a part of developing assertiveness and self-advocacy skills. In some areas, the transit companies have specially trained operators who are practiced in dealing with the needs of people with a variety of impairments; students in these areas should learn the procedures for reaching those operators.

TRIP PLANNING INFORMATION

Clerk number and/or name: _____

1. POINT OF DEPARTURE: _____
   (Place to catch bus/landmark)

Day: _____ Time(s): _____

Bus number(s): _____

###

2. TRANSFER POINT/LANDMARK: _____

Place to catch bus/landmark: _____

Time(s): _____ Bus Number(s): _____

###

3. TRANSFER POINT/LANDMARK: _____

Place to catch bus/landmark: _____

Time(s): _____ Bus Number(s): _____

###

4. DESTINATION: _____

Place to get off bus/landmark: _____

Time(s): _____

###

FIGURE 6.1 **Trip Planning Information Form**

##

5. POINT OF RETURN: _____

Place to catch bus/landmark: _____

Time(s): _____ Time of last bus: _____

Bus number(s): _____

##

6. TRANSFER POINT/LANDMARK: _____

Place to catch bus/landmark: _____

Time(s): _____ Bus Number(s): _____

##

7. TRANSFER POINT/LANDMARK: _____

Place to catch bus/landmark: _____

Time(s): _____ Bus Number(s): _____

##

8. DESTINATION: _____

Place to get off bus/landmark: _____

Time(s): _____

##

Students with low vision may avail themselves of printed transit schedules and maps to help in trip planning. Schedules are printed in fine print, so students need to use magnifiers, CCTVs, or close-focus monoculars to see them. Other ways to gather information include asking parents and friends who travel by bus. This is an acceptable avenue but should not be the only one. To be independent, students must be able to use all means of information gathering.

Sometimes the most efficient route is not obvious to a transit clerk because it may involve walking a few blocks to avoid an extra bus connection that might cause a trip to become more time-consuming. This kind of information comes through the grapevine of bus travelers or is developed through experimentation and trial and error. Sometimes it is necessary to mix and match transit systems to arrive at the most efficient mode. To get to an isolated destination, a student may need to take a major bus line and a paratransit bus or a major bus line and the rapid transit system. Operators are trained to give this type of information, but sometimes it is necessary to brainstorm with them to arrive at the best combination. It may also be necessary to call several transit systems to get all the necessary information.

It is a good idea for students to learn *key routes* that interface with a variety of other routes and transit systems. A key route is on a line that goes near the student's house and gives access to a primary urban area or central transfer points.

Teaching Bus Route Traveling

When the student has all the necessary information, he or she is ready to start traveling. As was mentioned earlier, there are a number of skills to learn in bus route travel, and they are taught in stages as the student becomes progressively more independent. Skills that are highlighted here are identifying the bus, choosing a seat on the bus, and identifying landmarks from the bus.

Identifying Buses

Students should have several means of identifying buses. It may not be sufficient to rely on the bus stop as the primary identifier, since several bus lines may stop there. If visual identification of the bus's route number is difficult or impossible with the unaided eye or monocular, the student must be prepared to ask questions of the driver to identify the bus. The most effective question is a *goal-directed question* that states where the student wants to get off the bus, such as, "Do you stop at Hilltop Mall?" Whenever possible, it is advisable to give a major landmark in addition to a street name because new drivers may not know all the street names, by asking, for example, "Do you stop at King and Santa Rita near the Goodwill store?" Most students who are reluctant to identify themselves as being unable to see enough to identify the bus will readily use goal-directed questions. Unfortunately, a student may be treated rudely if he or she asks the all-too-obvious question, "Is this the 52?" (which is not a goal-directed question) without saying , "I have a visual impairment and can't read the bus number." Goal-directed questions usually alleviate the possibility of being treated rudely or of getting the wrong bus.

Sitting on the Bus

When choosing a seat on the bus, students should be taught to bear in mind two primary considerations. First, which seat will enable them best to see the distinctive landmarks, such as a hill or large shopping mall, for their stop? Often this is a seat on the curbside of the bus. However, with seats that face the center of the bus, this may not be the case, or the major landmarks may be on the driver's side. A second question is, Which seat will place them in close proximity to the bus driver so that they may ask him questions? If both questions can be answered with one seat, all the better. On most buses, there is seating for the elderly and disabled at the front of the bus, but it may not always be unoccupied.

If there is no one seat that satisfies both conditions, sitting close to the driver is the more important consideration for students who are blind or visually impaired. Sitting close to the driver on the curbside may make the students more visible to the driver. This is an especially important consideration if they have asked the driver to tell them when they have reached the desired stop. If the students are out of sight, they may be out of mind. It can be helpful if they periodically question the driver by way of reminder, particularly during rush hours or if the driver is busy and hence more likely to forget them.

Identifying Landmarks

For students with low vision, it can be helpful to drive the route in a car during or just after the familiarization level to help identify landmarks and sequences of landmarks that occur prior to bus stops. The view will be slightly different in a car than from a bus, but in a car one may stop and repeat a segment of the route a number of times until the student is satisfied with his or her ability to identify landmarks or clues, such as hills or turns, that precede the bus stop.

Independent Travel

Once students are traveling at the independent level, the O&M specialist needs to focus on teaching them to prevent potential problems. Well-armed travelers have change for telephone calls and carry telephone numbers in case they get lost. In addition, they should agree with the specialist on a strategy for what to do in case they get on the wrong bus or get off at the wrong stop.

When a student has reached the independent level and is taking a solo trip, the O&M specialist needs to note the bus-identification number preparatory to following the bus in his or her car, so the bus can be identified in the tangle of traffic and at congested bus stops. The student and O&M specialist may maintain contact using long-range walkie-talkies that work within a two-mile range or by using cell phones.

Learning to travel on the bus is an important and major step in students' progress toward increased independence. With time and practice, they can become skilled and confident travelers, able to navigate the greater community more freely.

This chapter has examined the three primary domains in which students learn O&M skills. The next chapter focuses in more detail on techniques and methods for teaching the crucial O&M skills of orientation and cane travel.

Teaching Techniques

Teaching techniques are important vehicles of effective teaching. They can be learned, developed, and refined through imitation, experimentation, and trial and error. Orientation and mobility (O&M) specialists are exposed to diverse teaching techniques during their training, observations, and internships. It may not be until a specialist applies specific techniques, however, that their value in the teaching process is proved. Teaching techniques embedded in the teaching process prevent a haphazard approach to teaching. They form a legacy founded on accepted curricula and associated with the demonstrated attainment of skills by students. They are handed down from teacher to teacher in formal and informal settings. They can be gleaned from classes, demonstrations, and books. Regardless of their source, when applied, they invariably take on the stamp of the individual teacher and reflect his or her respective student population.

This chapter details diverse techniques and methods associated with the teaching and support of O&M skills in the various domains discussed in Chapter 6: home, school, and community. It focuses on the two fundamental areas of orientation and cane travel.

ORIENTATION

Without orientation skills, students who are blind or visually impaired may have knowledge of concepts and a variety of travel skills, but they will travel in a haphazard and inefficient manner. Orientation is a skill that makes it possible for them to travel purposefully and independently, to identify where they are at a given moment, and to maintain an awareness of where they are going. Some students learn to orient themselves with a minimum of assistance from the O&M specialist. The majority, however, profit from ongoing instruction in orientation in all the domains as they grow and mature.

Conceptual Bases of Orientation

Orientation is based in a knowledge of one's body parts and planes and their relationship to each other and their positions in space. It is further developed by learning to move in a purposeful manner with reference to objects and clues in the environment, and it is predicated upon the ability to recognize the structure of a sequence of landmarks.

The task of the O&M specialist is to encourage the student to focus on environmental information and to attach meaning to it. Much of this involves the purposeful hands-on experience of learning to identify and label sense-based information derived from textures, sounds, shapes, and smells. The O&M specialist can help the student to refine sensory perceptions and to learn to discern relevant sensory input.

Preschoolers have an insatiable appetite for information about the world. Children of all ages are naturally curious about the environment. Much of the learning environment is readily available, since the world naturally abounds in meaningful objects. However, there are types of learning experiences that need to be structured. Learning games can provide the necessary impetus to perform activities that need to be repeated to ensure that concepts are ingrained.

For example, teaching *laterality*, the recognition of right and left, can be an ongoing goal for years. It may start in preschool, if the teacher incorporates it into lessons from the beginning by labeling body sides and turns and by performing labeled coactive turns (turns in which two people move together, one guiding the other) with the student, all within the flow of lessons. In this case the teacher may gently manipulate the student's shoulders from behind as they both turn in the desired direction. The teacher announces, "Turn left" and then, "We are turning left" as they both turn left. This strategy enables the student to learn from their mutual movement.

Structuring Space

Learning about positional, directional, and spatial concepts is an integral part of developing orientation skills. Games can be played using sound to help to define the structure of space relative to the student's position. A ball with a beeper inside can be thrown, and the direction of the sound can be noted as it moves *toward* or *away* from the student, to the *right, left, in front, behind, above,* or *below.* The student who is blind can be requested to throw the ball *"straight ahead," "in back and to the right,"* and so forth or to throw the ball and to recount the path it took on the basis of the auditory feedback. Playing games with balls that beep (available from the American Printing House for the Blind, APH) can be exciting and fun. Games using sound help students to develop a grasp of the near spatial quadrants (such as *right front* or *left back*) relative to their bodies and to body movement (like *a quarter turn to the left*). A bell can be rung in a quadrant, and the student can be asked to label its position. The bell can be hidden within arm's reach of the student, and its position can be identified by the O&M specialist, *"The bell is to the right in front"* or *"The bell is to the near left in back of you."* Students will become adept at locating the bell and then ringing it. This can be a fast-paced game with lots of laughs.

Structuring Movement

Students who are blind, particularly those with spatial problems, also benefit from learning to structure their movement in a purposeful manner. Using sound-producing devices, such as a goal locator (available from APH), bell, or tape recorder, can facilitate learning to structure movement. Students can walk *toward* and *away* or *parallel to* a sound source that is moving or stationary. Ambient sounds may also be used for this purpose. When teaching *measured turns and facings* (such as quarter or 90-degree turns or about faces), O&M specialists may use sound sources, as well as stationary objects.

Students can learn to point purposefully to help them establish direction by having them lie on mats or align their bodies against a wall. The horizontal or vertical surface that they are in contact with gives them a concrete reference point upon which to base their movements. By starting them with their arms positioned next to their sides and, for example, giving the command, "Point to your right," students may then be directed to slide their arms and pointed fingers away from their sides until the arms reach a position that is continuous with the top plane of their shoulders. They may check this position tactilely with their left hands. They may also learn to hold their point and turn toward it (a quarter turn). (This technique is most effective when standing against a wall.) The surface against which they turn will delimit the turn accurately. With practice, students will learn the position of a right or left point and will be able to stand and point in free space and to point and turn toward their points, making accurate quarter turns. By combining two quarter turns, they may make a half turn or about-face. Eventually, they will internalize the feeling of measured turns and will be able to dispense with pointing.

From various fixed positions in a room, a student may retain orientation to major landmarks, such as the outside door or the sink, but when actually traveling to it, may veer off course or become distracted by obstacles. If the student takes a "sighting" by pointing to the known landmark and follows his or her point, he or she may more readily achieve the goal.

Projecting Movement into Space

With some students who are blind who have difficulty concentrating on the unfolding changes of direction involved in traveling a route, it is advisable to help them anticipate changes by questioning them in advance so that they must consciously label their projected movement. These questions promote a more conscious attitude toward their movement. For example, a series of questions and answers, which evolve in complexity as the student's skills develop over time, might sound like this:

1. Q. "To go to the chair in front of you, what do you have to do?"

   A. "Walk forward."

2. Q. "To go to the chair that is far right, what do you have to do?"

   A. "Make a quarter turn to the right and go forward."

3. Q. "At the T-intersection of the main and primary halls of the school, what do you have to do to get to Room 18?"

   A. "Make a quarter turn to the right, walk to the end of the hall, make a quarter turn to the right, and go straight through the door."

When giving students travel instructions, it is advisable to have them repeat them back to determine if they have assimilated and retained them. If students can retain a series of travel instructions, they will exhibit functional orientation to the degree that they follow the instructions. This is an important skill to develop and works much like the way motorists can travel in a strange area on the basis of directions they have solicited from gas station attendants.

If students are oriented to a car; can identify, from within and outside, which end of the car is the front; and have been told which way the car is facing (for example, toward the school on Dolan Drive), they will have a definite point of orientation from which to depart into the community. Facing the closed passenger door of the car, they know that to proceed into the community, they must make a quarter turn to the left, which puts the school behind them, Dolan Drive beside them on the right, and the next cross street in front of them.

Stationary Positioning

Students who are blind need to learn to retain stationary frontal positions when addressing focal areas and performing related activities. For example, students enter the room and locate their cubbies; must stand in front of the cubbies; and (1) temporarily store their canes, (2) remove their backpacks and store them, and (3) remove their jackets and store them. If the students twist around, sidestep, or back up significantly, they can lose their cubbies and may wind up putting their things in other students' cubbies.

Classroom Design

To assist students who are blind in learning to travel within the confines of their special education classroom for visually impaired students, the O&M specialist may consult with the classroom teacher regarding the design of the classroom. Teachers welcome this kind of "engineering" because it results in more efficient travel and hence shorter transitions and saved time within the classroom. It is best to structure the classroom away from large areas of open space where students may become disoriented and wander haphazardly. It is helpful to provide a continuity of trailing surfaces for direction taking or "corridors" to follow from one area to another. It is advisable to avoid arranging desks in horseshoe shapes, where students may become bottled up in the center. It is also helpful to place tape markers on the floors to indicate the position of the furniture so that when the custodians clean the room, the furniture may be returned to its original position. If furniture is off a foot or so, it can disorient a route traveler.

Maintaining Orientation

It is possible to teach students to deal assertively with problems of disorientation, so that when disoriented, they can retain control of the situation. If they learn to think of themselves as disoriented, rather than lost, and to think of their goal as recovering orientation, rather than being found, they will maintain a positive attitude with an emphasis on problem solving. Of course they may solicit aid if someone who can help is nearby. However, recovering orientation by other means allows students to maintain more responsibility for themselves.

A good rule of thumb for a student who is traveling a route and becomes disoriented is to return to the last known landmark and proceed from there. Initially, the O&M specialist may assist the student to return to the last known landmark by talking him or her to it or taking the student there using the human guide technique. However, with practice, this returning can become a reflexive response made by the student. Students can be taught to give themselves orienting prompts (for example, "The fountain is near the door; I must go toward it.") and to ask themselves orienting questions (such as "Where am I going after I get to the front door?" or "Which direction am I facing if it is morning and the sun is shining on my face?").

This strategy can also be helpful with students who have cognitive deficits or who take medications that dampen cognitive functioning, sometimes to the point that they forget what they are doing. An effective prompt for some students is *"STOP, LOOK, LISTEN, and THINK"* before going (or an appropriate modification addressing their sensory abilities). Students with cognitive deficits often become disoriented at junctures in routes where they must decide whether to continue straight or turn to the right or left. If they learn to "STOP, LOOK, LISTEN, and THINK" at such junctures, they are performing a series of problem-solving acts, the sum of which will help to orient them.

Students with low vision and cognitive deficits in power wheelchairs sometimes resort to traveling "on automatic" with little regard for where they are going. A self-orienting question for them is, "Where am I going?" This question helps them to focus on the task at hand, to abandon the automatic mode, and to take control.

Some students with cognitive deficits and low vision need help learning to discriminate among similar landmarks. For example, to them the concept of a *door* may take precedence over the unique collection of its properties. They need to be taught to use their vision, as appropriate, to isolate its properties to distinguish it from other doors. For example, is it a single or double door? Is it a doorknob or a handle door? What color is it?

Orientation Aids

A wide range of orientation aids is available to help students to understand and interpret space. These aids include auditory and large-print maps; the Chang Kit (used for creating tactile maps of limited spaces, available from APH); and similar tactile diagram kits, telescopes, and compasses. (See the Resources section for the sources of many of these products.)

The O&M specialist may need to make tactile maps for every school where there are blind students who have the established concepts to profit from their use. (It should be stressed, however, that maps cannot take the place of direct, hands-on experience of a location.) It also may be necessary to make tactile maps of the students' classrooms. In the case of self-contained classrooms for those with visual impairment, it is a good idea to make a map with modular pieces that attach and detach (for example, with Velcro) because classroom arrangements change over time. Making a map with modular pieces prevents the O&M specialist from having to start from scratch each time the room is changed. (For an in-depth discussion of making and using tactile and other types of maps, see Fazzi & Petersmeyer, 2001.)

As with all learning activities, the element of play increases involvement. It is possible to play mapping games in which students help to design the map in accordance with their classroom layout by placing missing pieces of "furniture" on it. When she was making a tactile map of her bedroom, one student told me that we needed *people*. I agreed, went out after school, and bought little plastic dolls with moving arms and legs. These people have become integral parts of most tactile mapping lessons, including those using the Chang Kit. Several small dolls have been fitted with canes made from matchsticks (with the heads removed) and toothpicks. In addition, lessons on inter-

A tactile map of the student's classroom, with furniture and little people, helps this student become better oriented and learn the routes to various goals in the room.

sections and traffic flow, with the Chang Kit, are a loss without toy vehicles. Miniature traffic signs are also helpful.

Large-print maps can be made by enlarging (and perhaps enhancing for visibility) existing print maps on an enlarging copier. Sometimes it is necessary to design and draw maps to build in necessary adaptations, to simplify, or to create individualized emphases for particular students. Maps of the classroom, school, neighborhood, or supermarket may be laminated and used with colored washable markers to trace routes and mark goals. Students may plot the routes on the maps before they start a trip or as they go along. This can be a valuable way for a student to learn to use a map and to translate real travel into a drawn line in two-dimensional space. Tracing routes with a colored

FIGURE 7.1 **A Student-Made Map**
This map was made by a student of the neighborhood around her school (OS). It is laminated so the student can trace routes on it with colored markers.

Playing with models with miniature vehicles, people, and traffic signs helps students understand traffic patterns and learn street-crossing skills while playing. These little traffic engineers created their own intersection!

marker helps the student develop mental mapping skills. It is important that the student orient the map to the cardinal directions, so that the map accurately reflects the relationship of the landmarks it describes. Travel directions may then be projected directly from the map into space.

Various optical aids can make maps more accessible. Magnifiers, a closed-circuit television (CCTV), or a close-focusing monocular can be used to view regular print maps. These aids are particularly helpful if the area to be studied is extensive and would otherwise require acres of paper to create a (resultantly unwieldy) enlarged version.

Braille and large-print compasses can be useful orientation aids for students who have the concepts to support their use. They are especially useful in situations in which the space is poorly defined or lacks distinctive landmarks, such as in large department stores, shopping malls, or neighborhoods where there are many similar landmarks. Compasses can be used in conjunction with maps to orient the map relative to actual space.

Students can use monocular and binocular telescopes to visually explore the space around them, to locate landmarks and to read street signs. Doing so enhances their knowledge of where they are by isolating landmarks that locate them within a space that is larger than one that is normally visually accessible to them. Telescopes may be used in conjunction with a map to help verify their position.

When students who use a cane and wear eyeglasses use a telescope (and a map), they discover that they do not have enough arms to wield their gear. With the addition of Croakies or a similar aid, their eyeglasses may be suspended around their neck, along with the telescope, or perched on their head, so they may alternately use their telescope. A cane may be tucked under the arm or stored in a cane holder or on the ground momentarily.

A well-equipped student: This girl uses a cane holder to store her cane while she uses her binoculars, which are suspended from a cord around her neck or kept in the case on her belt.

Orientation Markers

A student's environment may be marked with tactile and auditory markers to help the student recognize objects and maintain orientation. Braille and tactile labels may be applied to the student's cubby, desk, chairs, classroom doors, and so forth. Tactile markers should be of a consistent texture for each item assigned to a student and should be distinctly different from the texture assigned to another student who is blind; for example, one student may have velveteen, another terry cloth or synthetic fur. A tactile marker can be larger and thus is more rapidly identified than a lone braille label with the student's name, so it may be preferable for most items or may be paired with a braille label.

The outside of the student's classroom door may be distinguished by an auditory marker, in the form of a goal locator (available from APH), which is turned on during recess. For students who are blind, this continuing sound prompt provides a fixed reference point. Since it is reassuring, they may venture farther from the door out into the playground than otherwise, knowing that when the bell rings, they can discern exactly where to return.

Orientation to a New Site

Throughout their school careers, students will need to be oriented to new areas, including school, work, and commercial sites. Transitions can be eased if the O&M specialist takes time to familiarize and orient the students to the new areas prior to the transition.

O&M specialists should take a preliminary trip to a new site to familiarize themselves with it and go over it with a fine-tooth comb to isolate inconsistencies in numbering systems, architectural anomalies, and hazards. The next step is to familiarize the students to the general layout of the site, emphasizing the main buildings and routes with reference to a tactile or large-print map. Then follow-up visits are made to zero in on the location of specific rooms and areas. Students should be encouraged to study their version of the map between sessions to increase their familiarity with the site. The whole process may take numerous sessions. For secondary students who are mainstreamed and will be traveling to numerous rooms throughout the day, it is helpful to make a mock schedule (or get schedules early, when possible) and have them attempt to locate all the classes in the schedule. When the real schedule is established, they will be more familiar with the site and problem areas and problem-solving strategies.

Familiarizing a student to a new school using a map.

For some students it is necessary to take a less comprehensive approach to learning a site. Because of their disabilities, it may be necessary to focus on one route at a time until they learn it. Learning the whole schedule may take a semester. Until they have mastered the entire site, the students will rely on human guides or classroom aides to assist them.

When orienting students to commercial establishments, it is helpful to give labels to the different areas related to their specific characteristics or contents. For example, in a given supermarket, the front of the store may be identified by the presence of the doors and checkout stands, the back as the dairy section, the north side as the produce section, and the south side as the meat section. For young students and students with cognitive deficits, using these sections helps to alleviate the confusion that sometimes results from using the cardinal directions as labels. If students can identify that they are at the dairy end of an aisle, they can deduce which way to go to get to the front of the store where the checkout stands are.

Orientation skills are fundamental to all aspects of O&M, providing a foundation for efficient, purposeful travel at a variety of levels, and need to be taught in every domain. Each teacher will no doubt elaborate on and embellish the techniques for teaching orientation suggested here and originate some of his or her own.

CANE TRAVEL

In teaching cane travel, O&M specialists deal with some of the same questions that typically confront journalists who approach a writing assignment: *who, what, when, where,* and *how* (rather than *why*). *Who* qualifies as a candidate for cane travel training? *What* kind of cane should a student use? *When* should instruction begin? *Where* should it take place? *How* should it proceed? Of course, there is no blanket answer for any of these questions. The answers are as diverse as the students who qualify for O&M training.

Who Should Receive Cane Travel Instruction?

In considering which students would benefit from cane travel instruction, it is profitable to take a practical approach and ask several questions.

1. Regardless of the amount of usable vision a student has, will using a cane help him or her to travel in a safer, more independent, and more graceful manner than he or she is presently traveling? Students who are visually impaired but who have vision that can be measured with acuity charts sometimes slip through the cracks when students are being considered for cane travel training. They may navigate competently in the safe, known environments of home and school. However when questioned, their parents may report that they always hold hands with their children when they travel outside the home. Upon further assessment, it may be apparent that these students lack stereopsis and have absent or poor assessment of depth. They may also have marked visual field defects, especially of the lower quadrants of the visual field. These visual field defects can be evidenced by their head bobbing or continual looking down as they walk or by their use of foot- and/or hand-tactile means to explore the terrain in front of them if it is uneven or when there is a change of color or texture. They may also have night blindness.

Teaching such students to use a cane selectively, as they need it, produces a marked difference in their behavior, level of confidence, and degree of freedom. Their bodies will relax, their postures will improve, their pace will increase, and they will walk more confidently. They will learn to ascend and descend stairs independently using their canes.

Some students have good travel vision during the day but experience night blindness or, at least, have difficulty seeing in low light conditions and after dark. At these times, they need to travel with a human guide, or may rely on the chance passing of vehicles to illuminate their way or simply risk the perils of tripping, falling, and colliding with obstacles. Some, understandably, are reluctant to leave the house after dark, which can become a real restriction on their independence as they enter adulthood. Learning to use a cane can provide them with a useful adjunct to other means of facilitating night travel, such as the Wide Angle Mobility Light (available from Innovative Rehabilitation Technology; see the Resources section), or a powerful flashlight.

2. Is the student motivated to learn to use a cane? If a student has no desire to use a cane, there is little that the O&M specialist can do to teach the related skills. Teenage students with low vision, even when they are night blind and/or are rapidly losing their sight, may be reluctant to learn to use a cane because of the associated stigma and related issues of acceptance by their peers. Many students acknowledge a cane's utility, however, and consent to learn cane travel—although not necessarily to use a cane—if they are guaranteed seclusion from their peers during lessons. It is advisable to proceed sensitively, without ultimatums or hints of coercion. The O&M specialist can explore a cane's advantages with them and their parents and promote opportunities for them to meet adults who are blind who have a positive attitude toward the use of a cane. Learning to use a cane without making a commitment to use it at the end of training can be reassuring to students who are in the throes of losing their sight because they know that they will then have another strategy that they can choose to use in the future.

3. *Can and will the student hold a cane?* Some students, as a result of physical disabilities, are unable to hold a cane even with adaptations. For such students, other means must be explored for detecting objects and hazards, such as adaptive mobility devices (AMDs), curb detectors with wheelchairs, and various electronic travel aids (ETAs) (see Chapter 8). Some students with severe disabilities that affect their cognition and emotions may refuse to hold a cane or will use it in a manner that is hazardous to others. Attempts to train them may be fruitless or ill advised.

What Kind of Cane Should a Student Use?

Type of Cane

Several factors affect the choice of an appropriate cane for or by a student, primarily the student's size, age, and strength and the use to which he or she will put the cane. Students should be given the opportunity to choose among different types of canes through access to a cane library or local vendor. It may be advisable to choose a cane for a preschooler, however, since short sizes usually must be specially ordered.

A cane for a preschooler should be durable. A simple aluminum straight or rigid cane is preferable to fiberglass, which is more prone to break, and tiny shards of it can become embedded in the skin. However, if a student (of any age) has little hand or arm strength, it may be a good idea to use a fiberglass cane until his or her strength and endurance increase.

When preschoolers begin using a cane, they tend to push it in front of them. They also use it as a probe to explore the environment and to detect drop-offs. Refinements of technique come with time, sometimes much time. Because preschoolers initially tend to push the cane in front of them or, at best, to approximate a constant contact technique, it is important that the cane move smoothly on the ground. To facilitate smooth movement, the cane can be fitted with a marshmallow tip, mushroom cap, or roller tip, all of which allow the cane to slide with greater ease over irregularities of terrain (for sources, see the Resources section). When a cane catches too often in cracks, the student will resort to dragging it, holding it tentatively, or carrying it several inches above the ground, all of which reduce its effectiveness in detecting objects and hazards. A metal cane tip has greater sensitivity and may be preferable as a student's technique becomes more refined. Some people prefer metal tips to plastic tips. It is a good idea to allow students to choose the type of tip whenever it is possible and suitable.

A rubber grip with a flattened side is most useful for helping to orient the hand in a variety of positions during training. Canes with round handles tend to roll when dropped and can be difficult to retrieve. A cane with a crook handle, because of its fixed position, can be confusing to some students when they need to switch hands and may catch on the wrist when held in the nondominant hand.

Canes come in three principal styles: straight (also called rigid), folding, and telescopic. Straight canes tend to be the most durable and simple to maintain, but they are more difficult to store. Folding and telescopic canes have the convenience of shrinking to fit a limited space, but they are prone to disorders and require more maintenance and greater frequency of replacement. For preschoolers and those who are particularly hard on their canes, a straight cane is preferable.

Students who exhibit the hand strength and coordination to fold a cane can benefit from the versatility of a folding cane, which can be stored in a desk, backpack, pocket, cane holder, or any other limited space, such as in a car or on a bus. Folding canes improve the logistics of cane storage in classrooms, where canes may otherwise be stored on a rack or in a corner too far from their owners to be safe and convenient. They also provide a more convenient storage option when crowded conditions give rise to the possible hazard of tripping over straight canes that do not fit under students' desks or tables. A *heavy-duty* folding cane has the advantage of containing *two* elastic cords, so that if one breaks, the cane remains serviceable until it can be temporarily replaced and repaired. Lightweight folding canes have the disadvantage of having only one elastic cord. All folding canes should be maintained in their unfolded state when stored for prolonged periods to reduce the wear on the elastic cords, thereby promoting longevity. Students usually appreciate the advantages of owning a folding cane and look forward with excitement to getting their first one.

Telescopic canes are even more compact than their folding counterparts and, when made of fiberglass, are extremely lightweight and easy to store. However, they are prone to collapse and must be used with care. Otherwise they are excellent for selective use, to identify an individual as a person who is visually impaired, and for students who have low vision and/or night blindness and are sensitive about what they perceive to be the stigma of using a long cane.

Size of a Cane

In addition to the kind of cane, students need a cane of the appropriate size. Again, there is no neat formula for choosing the right size; however, several guidelines can be used. The cane must be long enough to clear the area that will be covered by the next step and to provide adequate reaction time in which to stop without jamming into an object or losing one's balance. The student's gait and rate of travel also need to be taken into consideration. A student with a rapid gait requires a longer cane because of the need for more time and space in which to react, while a student with a slow, shuffling gait requires a shorter cane. If a cane is too short, the student may tend to bend and stretch forward in an attempt to compensate. If the cane is too long, the student may hunch up the shoulder of the arm that is holding the cane or choke up on the cane, gripping it down on the shaft.

Because preschoolers are usually short and therefore need short canes, a problem can arise when teaching them to negotiate stairs: That is, the cane may be too short to reach the leading edge of the next step when descending without bending over and thereby compromising their balance. Teaching them to squat slightly will counteract the need to bend forward.

When Should Cane Instruction Begin?

There is no prescribed answer to the question of when cane instruction should begin because of the great variation in students and their needs, abilities and disabilities, self-concepts, the ages of onset of vision loss, and types of visual impairments. It is tempting to say "the sooner, the better" and in many cases this is true. However, students who are in denial about their disability and the need for cane travel will resist learning or may refuse to learn to use a cane. Others with degenerative conditions may wait until their ability to travel independently shrinks to a great degree before they agree to learn to use a cane. Still others, especially teenagers with low vision, will agree to learn but will use their canes only during lessons.

That said, given the proper motivation and the ability to hold a cane, the sooner training begins the better. Preschoolers readily take to a cane, and those who are blind often accept a cane as though they were welcoming a part of themselves that had been missing. They will use it as an extension of their bodies to explore the world around them tactilely and to create auditory feedback from the infinite variety of objects in their environment. You can actually witness the bonding process as a student accepts the cane. Sometimes it happens rapidly, and in other cases it is a gradual evolution.

There may be periods when a student rejects the cane or uses it so inappropriately that it must be taken away for a while. Students may purposefully or unconsciously brandish their canes, much like swords, threatening or injuring others in the process. These behaviors must be extinguished in the interest of safety, as in the following examples:

> One Chinese preschooler called his cane by a Cantonese word that, although the phonetic equivalent for the English word "cane," meant sword. He often used his cane much like a sword and as a club, despite the consternation and occasional injury of his O&M teacher. It took two years to shape his cane use away from his swordlike approach to a more acceptable approximation of a cane technique.
>
> * * * * *
>
> Shortly after being introduced to her cane, another young student took to brandishing it rhythmically above her head at unexpected moments, much to the peril of those who were close to her. She had rapidly bonded with her cane, so the problem was solved by depriving her of it for short periods following the brandishing episodes until the behavior was extinguished.

Where Should Cane Instruction Take Place?

To decide where to conduct cane instruction, the O&M specialist should consider the student's participation in each of the domains of home, school, and community. A student's life is lived out in the radiating circles of the domains, starting with home and expanding out through school, home and school communities, and the extended community. Cane instruction should take place in environments that will maximize age- and ability-appropriate skills in each domain.

How Should Cane Instruction Proceed?

Introducing the Cane

It is a good idea to begin cane instruction with a coordinated introduction of the cane to the student and parents or major caregivers. Sometimes parents or even members of the extended family need time to assimilate the concept of their child as a cane user. Sometimes negative attitudes and stereotypes about cane use must be counteracted through an educational process involving the major members of the family. The cane can be introduced in a positive way as a tool for enabling the student. For students with restricted visual fields, it is also helpful to emphasize that a cane can free them to use their vision for distance viewing, while the cane takes over the detection of nearby objects and obstacles. It is also possible to conduct a few joint introductory lessons for both the student and a parent. This shared learning experience can be an important step for both of them.

Building Strength

Students who are blind often lack hand and arm strength and may lack stamina. Consequently, it is frequently necessary to introduce a program of strength building to make it easier for them to manage their canes and to open and close heavy doors. Hand exercises should be included. A regular program may be instituted of lifting light weights to music or exercises to build shoulder girdle strength, such as performing the "wheelbarrow," in which students walk on their hands while the teacher or another student holds their legs up off the ground. For more information on this subject, it is helpful to consult an occupational or physical therapist.

An enjoyable way for young students to build leg strength and stamina is to ride tricycles. A blind student can ride a tricycle effectively at varying speeds while following a sound source, such as a beeping goal locator. In fact, some students travel faster and with more confidence and relaxation in this manner than with a cane.

Establishing Basic Patterns

The mechanical side of teaching cane travel is largely concerned with establishing motor patterns in general and, in particular, establishing *basic* motor patterns that can be shaped, refined, and built on. It is especially important to establish basic patterns with preschoolers and students with cognitive and motor and coordination problems. For example, *pushing the cane in front* can be expanded to *sliding the cane in front* or (on rough terrain, such as grass or gravel) tapping the cane in front. Tapping the cane in front can be expanded to *a rudimentary touch technique.*

Approaches to Teaching Techniques

Some students master various cane techniques rapidly with minimal exposure, but they are the exceptions. For the majority, the acquisition of cane skills takes time, sometimes years. It is advisable to tailor the pace at which skills are introduced to the individual by task analyzing each skill and teaching it in segments. As the student masters and becomes confident with each segment, a new aspect can be introduced. For example, using the touch technique and walking in step requires the performance of a number of separate skills:

1. appropriate grip

2. appropriate arm position for centering the cane

3. creating the arc by repeated flexion and extension of the wrist

4. maintaining a rhythm of one cane movement for each step

5. ensuring consistent coverage to clear a "path" the width of the body

6. walking in step so the cane clears the spot where the next foot fall will land

And these steps are only the beginning! Add to them the detection and negotiation of obstacles or drop-offs, the use of landmarks, and maintenance of orientation, and one confronts a staggering array of skills necessary to achieve the most commonplace goal of traveling to the bathroom or bus. Students become confused and overwhelmed if they are expected to perform too much too soon.

Similarly, it is often necessary to accept approximations of each skill. The pristine ideal of cane handling espoused by sighted practitioners quickly tarnishes in the real world of inattentive, boisterous, and uncoordinated children. It is often necessary to settle for a compromise between the O&M specialist's ideal and the student's lowest level of performance (or comfort zone), with the specialist continually challenging the student to refine or work above this habitual level.

It is a good idea to present training sessions on proper cane techniques to parents and other team members so they can reinforce these techniques with the student (see the section in Chapter 9 on Working with the Support Team). Then, when introducing a new cane technique to a student, it helps to share guidelines for prompting the technique with the team members who have been trained to support O&M. Sidebar 7.1 presents an example of a script for prompting the touch technique that was just analyzed. This script can be used as a teaching tool with parents and other members of the team who spend significant amounts of time with the student when he or she is traveling. The use of such scripts will promote consistent prompting and practice of cane skills for the student in a variety of environments when the O&M teacher is not present. (For more information about prompts, see Chapter 8.)

Coactivity

Using coactivity (physically assisting the student to achieve body positions and perform distinct patterns of motion) helps to implant motor patterns and to refresh them after they are introduced. Coactivity is especially effective in establishing cane position, movement, and coverage when teaching the constant contact technique to preschoolers. For the O&M specialist, it can be a profitable but backbreaking process. (It may help to sit in a wheelchair or other wheeled chair to slide around after a small student when working on flat surfaces or to use another long cane to coactively move the student's cane.) Coactivity may also be used for intermittent interventions to reestablish the appropriate performance of a technique.

Walking in Step

Too much emphasis on walking in step may throw off a student's gait. It is preferable to focus on coverage first or to accept adequate coverage as a compromise to walking in step. It may take several years to get from using an appropriate grip to walking in step. The full integration of the required skills may never be completed. For students with

**Sample Guidelines for Prompting
Cane Technique: Sliding or Touch Technique**

These guidelines describe the way to perform the sliding and touch techniques. They represent ideal techniques and, in practice, will be adapted to the student's ability as he or she grows into them. We will all be involved in helping to shape the student's safe cane travel. The *prompts* suggested here are questions you can ask to help the student learn to monitor his or her own cane use. The questions may change as the student's technique advances. To start with, though, the major concern is to make sure that the student moves the cane consistently from side to side in a wide-enough arc.

Grip
Hold the cane in the right or left hand and grasp the grip as though shaking hands, with the index finger pointing down the flat side. Think of the cane as an extension of the finger.

Prompt: "Is your index finger on the flat side?"

Hand/Arm
Ideally, the cane should be centered in front of the body with the arm relaxed.

Prompt: "Is your cane centered?"

Arc
Ideally, cane movement comes from movement of the hand, back and forth, like a door swinging on its hinges.

Prompt: "Is only your hand moving?"

Arc Width
Movement of the cane tip should encompass the space on the ground in front of the student one inch wider than the widest body part.

Prompt: "Is your arc wide enough?"

Rhythm
Ideally, the tip of the cane and heel of the opposite foot contact the walking surface at the same time in the touch technique. In the sliding technique, the cane tip reaches the outer edge of its arc as the heel of the opposite foot touches the ground. This ensures that "the cane touches last where the foot steps next," thereby clearing the path for each step in sequence.

Prompt: "Is your cane moving once for each step?"

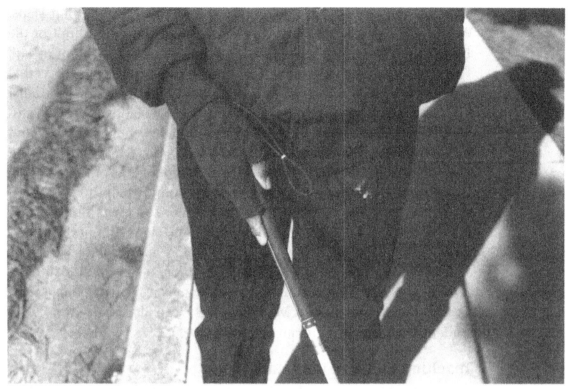

A proper cane grip, with the index finger pointing down the flat side.

severe handicaps, such as cerebral palsy and related gait problems, walking in step requires so much concentration that their gaits can become abnormal or more abnormal in the attempt. Their balance may also be thrown off. For others, attaining the skill is a matter of time and growth.

When a student's arc is well established, walking in step may be introduced. Coactivity is a standard approach to teaching this skill, but other methods of patterning motor skills can be used. For students with adequate vision, the O&M specialist may model walking in step using his or her own cane. An extension of this concept that may be applied to cane movement and coverage is to walk shoulder to shoulder in tandem and rhythm with a student, provided there is not too much difference in height between the two and the student can see well enough to match the specialist's pattern.

Another approach is to use verbal prompts to name the position of the cane as it reaches its respective right and left limits when describing an arc. For example, the O&M specialist can chant "open, shut" or "tick, tock" or "ding, dong" in time with the student's right and left steps. With a right-handed student, "open" designates the right limit of the arc or tap of the cane, whereas "shut" designates the left limit or tap. The student is taught to move the cane on command with the verbal prompts first. When the prompts are established, the O&M specialist asks the student to start walking, starting from a standstill. As the student steps forward with the left leg, the specialist chants, "open," and the student automatically taps on the right side; when the right leg steps, the specialist chants, "shut," and the student taps on the left side. Using paired prompts that are not terms of laterality helps to avoid confusing the opposing right-left patterns of upper and lower limbs. Using this approach, it is possible to talk students into step without their making a conscious effort. The approach helps to establish the feeling of a complex motor pattern to which they can direct their attention in time. As the pattern becomes conscious, students can chant to themselves and get themselves in step. Marching music can also be used to help a student establish a rhythm and stay in step.

Teaching Skills in Context

It is possible to teach cane techniques through an approach of repeated drills when a student has the maturity and cognitive level to benefit without becoming bored or frustrated. For the majority of students, however, a rote approach is the quickest ticket to inattentiveness. Moreover, for most students, skills taught in isolation are not retained or generalized to other situations.

By contrast, teaching skills in context, by reinforcing techniques as they are utilized within the flow of travel, avoids the deadliness of drills associated with teaching skills in isolation. Instead, patterns are established by coactive intervention or single repetitions over a long period. When a student is taught cane skills in the context of actual travel, he or she comes to appreciate the utility of a cane throughout the wholeness of the environment and across the endless varieties of space and terrain, while focusing on the rewards of exploration that come with traveling independently.

The Cane as a Tactile Tool

It is as important to give students—especially preschoolers and young students who are working at building tactile and auditory vocabularies and enriching their concepts of the world around them—time and

Using a cane to explore on irregular terrain.

opportunities to explore objects with their canes as it is to teach the acquisition of proper techniques. The reach of a cane goes far beyond the reach of a hand and arm. The cane's insensate qualities endow the student with greater courage to explore the unknown. It does not hurt to touch a cactus with one's cane, one does not get one's feet wet when a cane can be used to stir up a puddle, and no bruises are associated with reaching over the limits of a fence to see what lies on the far side. Thus, giving students a cane gives them a tool not only for travel, but for exploring the environment as well.

Promoting Cane Movement

The promotion of consistent cane movement is one of the major challenges to O&M specialists, much of whose career can be spent devising ways to transcend the perennial question, "Is your cane moving?" The ultimate responsibility for cane movement belongs to the students, but they often need help and reminders to stay on task and to make the connection between consistent cane movement and the effective detection of obstacles and hazards.

It is important to promote the concept of *being in control* through appropriate cane use. When students use their canes effectively, by keeping them in motion to clear the forward space, they keep themselves from colliding with objects and people and from tripping and falling. In this manner, they have control over their environment rather than being at its mercy. Some students move so slowly that they experience few negative consequences as a result of collisions and must be instructed about the awkwardness of their appearance as they gently crash through the environment. For some, this will be of little concern until they mature to a point where they are concerned with the image they project.

Cane movement is a motor habit that must be developed. Students can be helped to become aware of their lapses in cane movement and reinforced for consistent movement. For example, the O&M specialist can structure periods of cane travel in a safe, known environment, such as long hallways at school, during which he or she follows the student playing the student's favorite taped music. As soon as cane movement ceases, so does the music, and when the cane starts moving, the music resumes. It is also possible to seek or create obstacle courses in which students encounter unexpected obstructions at a greater frequency than normal and hence need to use their canes more vigilantly.

Competing Behaviors

Some cane travelers become adept at "echolocation," using reflected sound to tell them about architectural details and the qualities of the space around them. This is a useful skill and can be used to their advantage. However, the behavior is self-defeating if students use their canes as echo producers by tapping the canes up and down vertically, thereby losing the coverage of an arc. The sound reflected from the tapping cane tells the students only about the space around the upper part of their bodies and says nothing about the terrain, drop-offs, or low-lying obstacles. Inefficient tapping can become a strong competing behavior that may slow students down and put them at risk of accidents. Students can be taught to incorporate their tapping into the touch technique.

Echolocation may take other forms that compete with a student's ability to use a cane properly and to interpret cane feedback, as was the case with Jeffrey:

> Jeffrey, a fourth grader, came to school with enormous metal taps on his heels. He adjusted his gait to produce maximum sound. He could be heard from one end of the school to the other. In the process, auditory feedback, or echolation, took priority over the tactile feedback of his cane, and he lapsed into pushing his cane in front of him, which resulted in his bumping into low-lying obstacles and walking off the sidewalk. This evolution of focus from tactile to auditory feedback necessitated redoubled efforts by the O&M specialist to bring Jeffrey's focus back to his cane. The O&M specialist requested that the taps be removed from his shoes and then showed him less distracting ways of producing echoes by tapping his cane and by making mouth clicks. Jeffrey learned to integrate this echolocation feedback with the tactile feedback from his cane.

Competing behaviors may also take form in the development of idiosyncratic cane techniques, such as the one described next:

> One independent adult cane traveler developed the practice of trailing vertical surfaces by whacking her cane against the surface at waist level. This practice had a disastrous effect when she "trailed" a wall flanked by low-lying cement bicycle stands, which her cane failed to detect, leading her to trip and fall.

Teaching Route Travel

The ultimate goal of cane travel is for the student to travel safely, efficiently, gracefully, and flexibly. To attain this goal, many foundational skills need to be established, one of which is the mastery of route travel. Following and using a sequence of landmarks to achieve a goal and then to reverse the route to return to the starting point is an essential skill upon which flexible travel is built.

For students who travel within the confusing array of desks, tables, and learning stations of a classroom, it is essential to learn several basic routes to reach different areas in the room. A basic route may consist of traveling from the door, along the periphery of the room, to the circle-time area in the corner diagonally across from the door. The student learns to identify landmarks along the way. The entire route has the shape of an "L" or right angle. Next, by taking direction from various landmarks, the student may reach goals within the interior space of the room. Then the student may learn to travel routes that will enable him or her to move throughout the school to attain destinations in the daily schedule. In time, the student will come to know the space, ambient sounds, and layout of the school and will be able to travel flexibly without relying so heavily on the rigid sequencing of a series of landmarks. For students with cognitive and spatial problems, route travel will continue to be the surest means to attain goals.

To ensure that a student receives sufficient repetitions and uniform support while learning a route, it is a good idea to write a script that sets forth the verbal prompts so that everyone who works with the student on the route will promote the same behaviors in a consistent way. The verbal prompts are derived from a task analysis of the route during several dry runs with the student. It is always a good idea to work out any bugs in the script before the finished version is shared with others. Even then, changes may have to be made if problems arise and the script is incomplete or not working for some reason. A script card may be made by writing the script on a 5-by-8-inch index card that can be laminated with clear contact paper to prevent wear and tear. A plastic ring can be affixed and the script hung in a designated spot, so that the classroom teacher or aide (or any substitute for them) may use it until they commit it to memory.

Sidebar 7.2 presents an example of a script that was designed for Mary, a student who is blind and has multiple disabilities, who was learning the route from the bus to the bathroom and to her classroom. It includes both physical and verbal prompts. Mary had learned to go from the bus to the school entrance, but was having trouble with the segment from the entrance to the bathroom.

An additional challenge arose when Mary was unable to travel *straight* across the hall and veered to the right or left to such a degree that she either wound up in another hall or missed the bathroom door altogether. An additional script was designed to show the hierarchy of prompts for going *straight,* with fading built in (see Figure 7.2). The O&M specialist worked with the aide (who was to be Mary's primary support person for reinforcing mobility) until the aide had mastered

SIDEBAR 7.2 **Sample Route Script**

Route Script for Mary from the School Entrance to the Bathroom

Please use the words in the script (THOSE IN CAPS) and give the commands separately.

1. Just before she reaches the entrance:
   STOP WHEN YOU GET TO THE MAT.

2. When she has stopped, if her cane is in her left hand:
   SWITCH HANDS.
   (This builds in a physical prompt to turn right and trail the wall on the left after she crosses, thereby preventing her from turning left and going the wrong way.)

3. GO STRAIGHT ACROSS THE HALL.
   If she veers, start her again and give physical and verbal prompts for traveling straight. (Follow guidelines from PROMPTING HIERARCHY.)

4. When she has crossed the hall:
   TRAIL THE WALL ON THE LEFT.
   (Repeat the prompt as necessary.)

5. *After* she contacts the corner:
   GO AROUND THE CORNER AND WALK FOUR STEPS.

6. When accomplished:
   SQUARE OFF.

7. When accomplished:
   SWITCH HANDS.

8. When accomplished:
   GO STRAIGHT ACROSS THE HALL.
   (Same instructions as Step 3.)

9. When accomplished and she contacts the wall:
   FIND THE BATHROOM TO THE LEFT.
   Reinforce the prompts for a while; then gradually fade them until Mary is independent.

the two scripts and the prompting and fading techniques. Consequently, Mary learned the skill and concept of traveling *straight* across the hall. She also mastered the entire route to such a degree that she learned to travel more flexibly and to incorporate segments of the route into other routes and to find the bathroom from a variety of locations within the school. (Further discussion of different types of prompts appears in Chapter 8.)

Levels	Examples	Reward
1. Full physical ———————→	Both hands on shoulders all the way.	"I like how you went straight across the hall."
with		
Full verbal ———————→	"Go straight across the hall."	
2. Partial physical ———————→	Both hands on shoulders for half the crossing, with repeated trials gradually fading to one-quarter of the way and finally to an initial prompt only.	"I like how you went straight across the hall."
with		
Full verbal ———————→	"Go straight across the hall."	
3. Fade physical with		
Partial verbal ———————→	"Go straight"	"I like how you went straight across the hall by yourself."
4. Partial verbal ———————→	"Go."	"I like how you went straight across the hall by yourself."
5. No prompt ———————→	Silence.	"I like how you went straight across the hall by yourself."
6. No prompt ———————————→		Silence. Student receives natural consequences of having functioned independently.

Be sure to pull back prompts as the student shows initiative. Hold off making verbal prompts once the pattern is established to see if the student initiates behavior, such as spontaneously switching hands or stopping to square, without them.

FIGURE 7.2 **Prompting Hierarchy for Teaching Mary to Walk Straight Across the Hall**

Cane Miscellany

The Cane Library

Maintaining a cane library facilitates the assignment of canes to students. A working cane library should have at least one of every size available, proceeding in 2-inch increments from the shortest straight canes for preschoolers to the longest canes, in various types, for young adults. It is even better to have two or three in each size to use as backups when canes are damaged, lost, or need repair or when several students are using the same size. It is also good to have a range of types of canes available for sampling and to give students choices. Ultimately, the size of the library depends on the resources available for obtaining canes and the size of the cane-using population that one is serving. It is possible to ask parents to buy their child's first cane and thereafter to trade up from the stock in the library. If a student is particularly hard on canes, his or her parents may be recruited to subsidize the purchase of canes, if they have the resources. A library may start out small and grow in time.

Since long canes come in a great variety of makes, types, and sizes, they may be organized for easy access by storing them according to length. Folding canes will last longer when stored in their open state to minimize wear on the elastic. Canes may be hung open on a wall, in order of their respective lengths, from a series of flexible clips (the kind used to hang tools and brooms) that are available at a hardware store. They may be hung side by side from the shortest to the longest with adjacent labels indicating lengths.

Cane libraries can be organized much like a book-lending library with a checkout card assigned to each cane. Canes may be marked on the shaft or tip with an indelible marker, stating the school district initials, type of cane, size, and an identification number, if there are more than one of the type and size. When a cane is added to the inventory, a checkout card is made up with a description of its type, length, and number, and space to record the teacher's and student's names is included, along with the location (usually the student's school or home if the student is assigned a backup cane) and the checkout and return dates (see Figure 7.3).

It is also helpful to maintain an overall inventory of all the canes in the library to help prevent shortages. Figure 7.4 illustrates a form for documenting each cane according to whom it is loaned to, its type,

Choosing a cane from the cane library.

Ambutech Folding Cane			42" #3
Dates		Teacher/Student	Location
Out	In		
8/00	9/01	N. Knott/Keith Wilson	Cherry Valley
8/01		N. Knott/Amber Martinez	Woodrow

FIGURE 7.3 **Sample Cane Checkout Card**

					Date		New Cane
CANE INVENTORY							
Student	Cane Type	Length	Condition	Tip	Out	In	Ordered

FIGURE 7.4 **Cane Inventory Form**

length, condition, tip, when checked in or out, and whether another of the same size needs to be ordered. This form is best kept in pencil so that changes in status may be indicated when needed.

Cane Maintenance

In addition to the canes themselves, it is necessary to keep a variety of supplies on hand in the cane library for maintenance purposes (see Sidebar 7.3). It is essential to have a ready supply of cane tips in various sizes and types, including roller, marshmallow, and mushroom tips and straight plastic and metal tips. Other supplies include Scotchlite reflective tape for making canes visible at night, which often needs to be replaced because of the punishment it takes being at the receiving end of the cane. Heavy-duty epoxy glue is useful for gluing on tips when necessary. Wax or soap is helpful for lubricating stubborn joints on folding canes. Steel wool may also be used to smooth joints. A small vise that can be mounted onto a table is essential when sizing canes with a pipe cutter. A vise is also useful for removing stubborn cane tips, with the help of pliers, and for assisting in the straightening

---

SIDEBAR 7.3 **Supplies for Cane Maintenance**

- ❏ cane tips in various sizes and types:
  - ❏ roller tips
  - ❏ marshmallow tips
  - ❏ mushroom tips
  - ❏ straight plastic tips
  - ❏ metal tips
- ❏ Scotchlite reflective tape
- ❏ heavy-duty epoxy glue

- ❏ wax or soap
- ❏ steel wool
- ❏ vise
- ❏ pipe cutter
- ❏ pliers
- ❏ retractable razor knife
- ❏ heavy-duty fabric tape
- ❏ Allen wrench

---

of bent canes. A retractable razor knife is useful for removing glue from cane tips, when changing from a marshmallow tip back to a straight tip, and for paring down straight cane tips that are too large to fit into existing marshmallow tips. Heavy duty fabric tape can be used to reinforce straight tips (to which marshmallow tips have been attached) above the joint. This is advisable if the student gives his cane a real beating because it reduces the tendency of the straight tip to snap in two. Heavy-duty fabric tape may also be used as an alternative to gluing to ensure that a marshmallow tip fits snugly around a straight tip by wrapping the straight tip prior to installing the marshmallow tip. When using canes with crook handles, it is important to carry an Allen wrench, in the appropriate size, or to give one to the student, to tighten the handle whenever it loosens.

The techniques discussed in this chapter for teaching the skills of orientation and cane travel will apply to most students who are blind or visually impaired. However, teaching O&M skills to students who have other disabilities in addition to their visual impairments usually requires different approaches and techniques than those already described. Chapter 8 discusses ways to work with students who have multiple impairments.

Students
with Multiple Disabilities

Teaching students who are blind or visually impaired and have additional disabilities draws upon the deeper reserves of knowledge and creativity of an orientation and mobility (O&M) specialist. All students are different, and the presence of additional disabilities increases their individual uniqueness. No single formula exists that can be neatly applied to the broad spectrum of students with visual and multiple disabilities. Often the most important single attribute that an O&M specialist can bring to bear on a given teaching challenge is attitude. Working with students with multiple disabilities and their families necessitates a wide-reaching attentiveness, openness, and willingness to go the extra mile. With such an attitude, an O&M specialist's efforts can have positive and rewarding results.

The first part of this chapter summarizes some broad guidelines for working with students with multiple disabilities. The second part addresses techniques and methods of working with students who are blind or visually impaired who use wheelchairs and those who have communication disorders.

GENERAL GUIDELINES

A number of general recommendations can be made about working with most students who have other disabilities in addition to visual impairments. It is usually helpful to break down techniques into simple parts, emphasize consistency and repetition, tailor instruction to the individual student's needs, and make sure that everyone who works with the student understands how to reinforce the O&M skills that are being taught. These are suggestions that may be generalized to cover a broad range of students with multiple disabilities. However, not all suggestions apply to all students. Some of the suggestions offered here are presented in more detail elsewhere in this book, and references are given to other chapters where each topic is discussed.

Use task analysis. In task analysis, complicated tasks are divided into their component successive steps, or subskills, which can then be taught one at a time. Task analysis enables the student to experience mastery of each subskill before he or she attempts the entire task. The route script presented in Chapter 7, written to help Mary travel from the school entrance to the bathroom, is an example of task analysis.

Teach skills within the context of a student's daily routine. Embedding the teaching of skills in the flow of students' everyday activities helps to capitalize on students' intrinsic motivation because they learn the functions of the skills in the meaningful context of real life. It also promotes repetition and encourages generalization of skills. (See the section on Promoting Functionality in Chapter 5.)

Tailor prompts to the individual student. Prompts, or directions to a student to perform a particular skill or action, can be of different types—ranging from various ways of physically manipulating or encouraging the student to simple verbal reminders—and are administered at different levels of intensity according to the student's abilities and needs, as described in Sidebar 8.1. The type and level of the prompt should be tailored to the individual student and then faded as the student's skill increases. An example of a prompting hierarchy, in which the level of prompts is gradually decreased and finally faded altogether, appears in Chapter 7 in the section on cane travel.

Provide consistency and adequate repetitions. Make sure that everyone who works with the student uses consistent language to describe skills, techniques, concepts, and so forth to minimize opportunities for confusion. In particular, using scripts within a structured learning situation that is repeatedly presented to the student supports maximum retention of what is taught. See the section on The Use of Language in Chapter 5 and Teaching Route Travel in Chapter 7.

Use a flexible and functional approach to teaching skills. Individual students may be unable to learn skills based on the logical hierarchy of

SIDEBAR 8.1 **Prompting Levels**

*P*rompts, or the teacher's directions to the student to perform a particular skill, range in level from physical manipulation to guide the student through the skill to minimal verbal reminders. The goal is usually to fade, or gradually diminish, the level and intensity of the prompt until the student is performing the activity independently. The following are levels of prompts, from most to least intrusive:

* *Coactive or hand-over-hand prompting.* The O&M specialist provides continuous physical input by helping to move or guide the student through the movement or activity. This level of physical guidance can be helpful, for example, in teaching a student how to move the cane as he or she learns to make an arc while walking.

* *Isolated physical prompt.* The O&M specialist touches the student intermittently to produce a physical directive to promote a particular movement or activity, as in the example of Karin:

  > Karin starts to veer to the left when crossing an open space. If she maintains her veer, she will not attain her goal. The O&M specialist taps her lightly from behind on the left shoulder to signal that she needs to adjust her line of travel to the right.

* *Object prompting.* The O&M specialist touches or moves an object the student is manipulating (or failing to manipulate), such as the cane, as in this example:

  > While traveling down the hall, Angus becomes distracted as he passes an outside door from which playground noises are coming. He stops moving his cane from side to side but continues walking toward a pole that divides the fire doors ahead of him. His O&M specialist steps up and starts to move his cane for him briefly and without touching Angus. Her action brings Angus's attention back to his cane and the work of keeping himself safe by moving his cane in a protective arc.

* *Gesturing or modeling.* The O&M specialist physically demonstrates an activity for a student to imitate. With students who have sufficient vision, the observation may be visual. Others may need to observe physically by placing their hand or hands so that they may feel the movement the specialist is demonstrating, as was the case with Audra:

  > Audra has never opened a door with a lever opener. Her O&M specialist tells her to place her hand on top of his as he demonstrates manipulating the lever to open the door. In this manner, Audra feels his movement as he physically models operating the lever. She then attempts the task by herself, imitating his gesture.

* *Verbalization.* The O&M specialist tells the student what to do or gives limited verbal prompts to encourage an activity.

an O&M curriculum and may need to forgo or skip certain levels. It is therefore necessary for the O&M specialist to adopt a flexible approach that is aimed at helping the student accomplish a desired task, rather than learn a designated set of skills. Some students may also not be able to perform skills in an ideal or traditional manner but may be able to accomplish a task in an adapted or alternative way. For example, Joey, a kindergartner, could not flex his wrist and resorted to using the larger muscles of his arm to sweep his cane from side to side in an arc. Julie learned to squat as she descended stairs so that her cane would touch the tread of the next step or the landing.

Some students may use adaptive mobility devices (AMDs), which are devices that promote safe and independent travel for students who may be unable to use a long cane at first. An AMD is constructed to give full frontal coverage and to maintain continuous contact with the ground. (For a discussion of AMDs and illustrations, see Farmer & Smith, 1997).

Use reverse chaining. Reverse chaining is similar to task analysis or the teaching of subskills before having a student put an entire task together. It involves teaching a skill or a travel route in a piece-by-piece manner, starting with the last segment (or link of the chain), the one nearest the goal. Each preceding segment of the route is taught and connected to the succeeding links as the student masters it. The end result is that the student puts all the links together and travels independently from the point of origination to the goal. Some students learn more readily using reverse chaining because they have the encouragement of reaching the goal with each trial.

Provide short sessions with increased frequency. Short sessions allow for some students' decreased attention span or lack of endurance, while more frequent sessions provide maximum opportunities for learning.

Provide community-based instruction. When the O&M specialist can schedule teaching time within an existing community-based program, he or she can take advantage of meaningful and motivating group activities, such as on-the-job work training, shopping, or leisure pursuits like bowling or aerobics at the "Y."

Train a staff member who is familiar with the student. Some students work most productively with an adult with whom they already have a comfortable, consistent daily relationship. When this person is taught to reinforce various O&M skills on a daily basis under the supervision

Some students may need to perform skills in an adapted way, such as squatting when descending stairs so the cane can reach the ground.

of the O&M specialist, the student may be more likely to learn. This person is especially important if the O&M specialist is scheduled on a weekly basis or even less frequently.

Network with the support team. It is critical to emphasize O&M goals and objectives with all members of the support team so that they are all able to reinforce specific learning behaviors in a consistent fashion. Networking provides for maximum support and reinforcement of O&M skills and techniques in all the domains and at times when the O&M specialist is not present. Maintaining close contact with the parents is especially vital. (See Working with the Support Team in Chapter 9.)

These suggestions are useful in working with most visually impaired students who have additional disabilities. There are other groups of students with extremely low-incidence disabilities that require additional specialized knowledge beyond these general points and that may not have been treated in depth in some O&M training programs. In particular, O&M specialists will find it helpful to have some knowledge of how to work with students who use wheelchairs and students who have limitations in their abilities to communicate.

STUDENTS IN WHEELCHAIRS

Of all the information presented in this book, this section on visually impaired students in wheelchairs is the one I needed most when I completed my internship and stood, certificate in hand, facing my first O&M caseload. Students who are visually impaired or blind are a low-incidence population, and those in wheelchairs represent an even smaller segment of this population. Consequently, little had been presented about them in the university curriculum for O&M specialists, and little was available in the literature of the field. Although many of the basics of teaching O&M can be applied to teaching students in wheelchairs, the O&M specialist may need to learn more about the mechanics of the wheelchair the students use and the safety issues associated with wheelchair use. For an additional discussion of concerns related to students in wheelchairs, see Rosen, 1997. Information about local vendors of wheelchairs or other supplies can usually be obtained from a student's physical or occupational therapist.

The demands of my caseload and the paucity of my information impelled me to do further research about wheelchair use. The material in this section represents diverse gleanings from conversations and correspondence with physical and developmental therapists, mentors and colleagues in the field of O&M, rehabilitation engineers, friends with wheelchairs, students, and parents of students. It also reflects applications and solutions to challenges I have worked through with my students while teaching them. I have found that, as in all teaching, keeping an open-minded, eclectic, and experimental attitude is essential.

Types of Wheelchairs

Students are matched with a variety of wheelchairs, each one reflecting the owner's individual needs and abilities. Many students in wheelchairs in special education classes are quadriplegic and have various degrees of limitations in the use of their hands and arms. Those with little arm strength and use are natural candidates for power chairs. Some students rely solely on manual chairs: two armed, one armed, or lever armed. Some make the transition from manual to power chairs, and still others trade back and forth as the situation dictates. Another option is a manual chair that is convertible to power and is operable in either mode with a few adjustments by an attendant. Regardless of the type of wheelchair, some students require attendants to assist them with a variety of tasks throughout the day. In the school setting, these duties are usually performed by specially assigned classroom aides and teachers.

Wheelchair Safety

Safety is an essential and ongoing consideration when working with students in wheelchairs. Without proper protection, training, and supervision, students can injure themselves and others. I learned this when I started working with my first student in a wheelchair:

> Rachel, a fourth grader, had just obtained a quadra, which is a lightweight manual wheelchair. She was also being evaluated for a power chair. When the power chair arrived, some team members regarded it with skepticism. They voiced two major fears: "She'll injure herself" and "She'll injure other children."
>
> One weekend while playing in her new power chair with her sister and dog at the playground, Rachel "ran" across the blacktop and smashed into a pole, badly injuring her foot. This incident filled Rachel with apprehension about the chair and reinforced the skepticism of the team. She didn't use her power chair again for months. Her developmental therapist responded to the situation by having a footrest designed that held her feet in flexion and kept them from sliding into a vulnerable position. This footrest protected her feet from unexpected collisions. The incident also underscored the need for appropriate supervision.
>
> Around the same time another alarming event occurred. A man known to Rachel's family tipped his wheelchair over a two-inch drop-off and hit his head. Several days later, he went into a coma and died of a cerebral hemorrhage. This incident was deeply disturbing to all the people who loved and worked with Rachel, especially her parents. "What price, independence?" was the question on everyone's lips. Until that time, the parents had viewed the wearing of a protective helmet as unnecessarily stigmatizing. In response to the situation, the developmental therapist obtained an attractive, blue, soft helmet

that was accepted gladly by all. Rachel resumed using her power chair with her feet and head protected.

The aim in highlighting the dangers and pitfalls of wheelchairs is not to discourage the teaching of O&M to students who use them, but to champion safety. Without belaboring the point or recounting many other incidents of pedestrian and wheelchair accidents resulting in broken feet, injured legs, and associated injuries, suffice it to say that the specter of injury is always present, and O&M specialists, students, and the support team must bear this possibility in mind and guard against it continually.

The O&M specialist is in a unique position to enforce safety with students who could be dangerous to themselves and others. Students are frequently assigned power chairs with minimal preparation for the challenges of driving with low vision. They are not required to take driver's education or to pass a driving test. The O&M specialist may be the first person to address the critical issues of driving with reduced acuity, lack of depth perception, photosensitivity, poor fixation, limited or defective visual fields, and reduced reaction time. This is a significant responsibility.

There are several ways the O&M specialist can buttress his or her efforts to teach safe travel. One is to ensure that the student is equipped with the appropriate physical devices that enhance safety. Two other ways are training the support team and promoting environmental adaptations.

Physical Safety Devices

Helmets provide head protection in the event of a chair's tipping over. Wheelchairs are especially vulnerable to minor drop-offs, such as sidewalk margins (often hidden by grass obscuring the change in level). More severe drop-offs include stairs, curbs, potholes, and wheelchair lifts on buses and vans. Helmets come in a variety of types and styles. Some are attractive or stylish enough to suit the most particular student. They can be purchased through specialty catalogs and at cycle shops.

Foot bracing provides protection for feet by creating a support that holds the feet firmly in place, thus preventing them from slipping and dangling. It also acts as a bumper, providing a margin of forward and lateral protection. Foot bracing can be obtained by physical and developmental therapists.

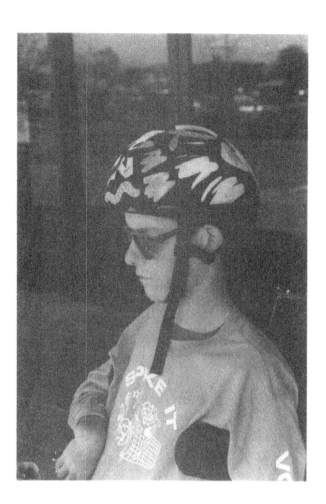

A helmet is essential to protect a student if a wheelchair tips over. Students will wear helmets more willingly if they are able to choose an attractive one.

Curb detectors, when attached to a wheelchair, give auditory warning of contact with obstacles to the front and sides. They provide a measure of reaction time in which to stop or change course, so that students do not collide with obstacles. Students may use them to trail vertical surfaces. They may be installed with thumb screws so that they may be easily removed and reattached. This is advisable because the tips of the detectors can damage furniture and walls in a student's home. Curb detectors can be purchased at auto supply stores.

Gloves protect the hands from the injury of a lateral impact (such as scraping along a vertical surface) while propelling a manual chair.

Seat belts are standard equipment on wheelchairs, but they deserve mention because some students prefer not to use them or to wear them so loosely that they provide minimal support. Seat belts should be checked periodically and kept securely fastened.

Seat belts are essential safety gear for wheelchairs.

Power-level controls are toggle switches on the controller box of power chairs that control the speed. Some have indoor and outdoor high and low levels. Outdoor high can be as fast as nine miles an hour, which is considerably faster than a standard 3-mile-an-hour walking pace. Some switches can be adjusted by the student at will, but sometimes this autonomy presents risks, especially among teenage students who may enjoy peeling out, doing wheelies, and speeding. Sometimes training in safety and limit-setting are not sufficient to prevent reckless driving.

A simple intervention is to apply heavy-duty fabric tape to the switches to hold them in the desired level or, in the case of outdoor high, to "off." However, it can be inconvenient to do so if the levels need to be adjusted by the student or attendant for street crossings or hills. A more involved but effective intervention is to limit the speed on computerized chairs by accessing the performance adjustment menu. The operating instructions manuals explain how to access this menu, although warranties may not be honored if it is done by unqualified persons. On some chairs that are not computerized, a speed-limiting device can be installed by the vendor that makes it possible to adjust the range of speed minutely beyond and between the basic high and low speeds. Such a device is accessible from beneath the controller. The student may ask the attendant to adjust it appropriately.

Hill-stopper brakes are devices that can be installed on manual chairs. When applied, they prevent the chair from rolling back, enabling a student with limited strength to work his or her way up a hill without losing any ground or having to rely on strength alone to keep from rolling back down the hill. For some students, this is the only way to travel independently up a grade. Hill stoppers are applied prior to climbing a hill by operating small levers similar to brake levers. Any student who can operate brake levers can apply hill stoppers. They are available through wheelchair vendors.

Safety and the Support Team

As was noted previously, the time spent in formal O&M instruction is a relatively small segment of a student's life. Therefore, it is important to promote safety by developing a network of people who consistently reinforce the same safety issues with the student outside O&M lessons. Such a network is especially important with students who have cognitive deficits, who may need more supervision and more frequent reinforcement to retain such messages. The safety network consists of the entire support team—including classroom aides, teachers, parents, bus drivers, and other specialists who work with the student.

The O&M specialist can schedule individual and group training sessions with members of the support team to highlight specific safety issues. Safety guidelines should be written for each student and distributed to each team member, and copies should go into the student's files. The written guidelines become a mutual reference point when discussing or reinforcing specific issues. An example of such guidelines is presented in Figure 8.1. The O&M specialist may also need to monitor the student's travel activities with members of the team. Monitoring may involve accompanying the student and aide (or others) on trips around the school and into the community.

Additional information that is important to give teachers, aides,

SAFE COMMUNITY TRAVEL GUIDELINES
FOR JOHN FOX

John has LOW VISION and DOES NOT SEE WELL. He also REACTS SLOWLY and is INATTENTIVE at times. Therefore, he can put himself and others in danger. He has injured others seriously and has injured himself by tipping his chair over. To avoid injuries, he must

1. always wear his helmet when traveling.

2. always be supervised one on one during outdoor travel and when in an environment that is unknown or hazardous. Hazards include

<table>
<tr><td>curbs</td><td>drop-offs</td></tr>
<tr><td>stairs</td><td>low-lying obstacles</td></tr>
<tr><td>uneven ground</td><td>traffic</td></tr>
<tr><td>poles</td><td></td></tr>
</table>

3. always travel at low speed (switch toward him).

4. always keep his head up and eyes open when traveling.

5. always slow down for pedestrians or stop when unsure.

6. always stop at blind corners and then go slowly.

7. always announce "I'm backing up" before backing up.

If we all support these safety procedures with John, he will not injure himself and others, and he will become a better traveler.

Thank you,

Natalie Knott
Orientation and Mobility Specialist

_222-1822_
Telephone number

FIGURE 8.1 **Sample Safety Guidelines for Wheelchair Travel**

and other important people during training sessions is outlined in Sidebar 8.2. It is helpful to give them guidelines in printed form, such as this, so they may follow along as you present the information in training sessions and can keep them for future reference. The guidelines presented in this sample handout are quite general and explain issues relating to people with visual impairments as well as people in wheelchairs, since many people who work with a student may be unfamiliar with both.

Safety and the Environment

The O&M specialist can help to promote safety by exploring the student's home and school environments in the company of the student's parents and teachers. In many cases, safety is a matter of common sense and reinforcing concepts of intervention and close supervision in risky areas. In some cases, adaptations are necessary to promote safety or enhance accessibility. Is the fire-drill route accessible to students in wheelchairs? Does it need to be ramped? Are curb cuts necessary for a safe, speedy, and independent exit?

In situations in which the environment needs to be made accessible or altered in some way for safety reasons, the O&M specialist and/or the student (as appropriate) can act as advocates, using their influence to bring about changes, as in this example:

One O&M instructor became concerned about her student's safety after the student acquired a power wheelchair, so she wrote the following letter to her supervisor, and sent copies to the principal, the classroom teacher, and the teacher of visually impaired students:

I am writing regarding safety issues concerning Anna Marcos's mobility at Jorge Gonzales High. She has acquired a power wheelchair recently, and although she is making good progress in learning to use it under supervision, she is at significant risk because of her visual impairment. She cannot detect drop-offs because she lacks stereopsis, which affects her depth perception. I am requesting that several adaptations be made to make potential hazards more visible to her:

1. Paint an eight-inch yellow stripe around the quadrangle to provide a distinct visual clue that there are stairs going down.

SIDEBAR 8.2 Suggestions for Working with a Student Who Is Blind or Visually Impaired and Is in a Wheelchair

1. When approaching the student or entering a room where she is, say something, if only a word, to let her know of your presence. If you are unfamiliar to her or she does not yet recognize your voice, let her know who you are. For example, "Hello, Karen, it's Ms. Black." It is also important to tell the student when you walk away or leave the room, so that she will not be left in the position of talking to someone who is not there.

2. When escorting the student into a strange setting, tell him in a quiet voice where things are in the room and who is there, so that he can feel more comfortable.

3. When it is necessary to move the student, when performing a transfer or when pushing her in her wheelchair, announce your intentions prior to moving her. For example, "Kati, I am going to assist you out of your wheelchair, so you can spend some time on the mat." This type of communication helps her to anticipate things she cannot see, such as your approach, and puts her in the position of feeling more like an informed participant and less like an object being manipulated. Talk the student through each step of the movement, so she can anticipate the actions and ultimate outcome.

4. When talking to the student, it is important to be concrete and specific when designating the positions of objects and obstacles relative to his position.

   For example, say:
   "To your right."
   "To your left."
   "Directly in front of you."
   "Next to your right foot."
   "To the right of your head."

   Rather than
   "Right here."
   "Over there."
   "This way."

5. When referring to the position of the student's wheelchair relative to various objects, obstacles, or architectural details, be specific in relating its parts to the environment. For example, "There is a chair in front of the right wheel of your wheelchair." If the student cannot figure out how to negotiate this obstacle, verbalize how he must move his chair to negotiate it one step at a time. For example, tell the student, "Back up." After he backs up, tell him, "Make a quarter turn to the left." When he does so, say, "Go forward a little," then, "Make a quarter turn to your right," and then, "Go straight" until the entire maneuver is accomplished.

6. Communicating in concrete terms that describe the position of objects in relation to the student's position in space will help her to form an inner image of the environment. This inner image will enhance her motor planning and help her to make correct movements to negotiate the chair, allowing her to feel less helpless and dependent and to gain a greater sense of control over her movement in the environment.

2. Paint eight-inch yellow stripes at the top of each set of stairs in the building for the same reason.

3. Paint black-and-white stripes, at the eye level of a child seated in a wheelchair, on the aluminum dividers of all double doors. The doors become invisible under lighting conditions that produce glare, and Anna crashes into them.

There is another safety hazard that affects Anna, although it isn't related to her visual impairment. The fire exit from her main classroom is unsafe and inadequately accessible to her. There is a discrepancy in levels at the base of the ramp. They need to be evened to prevent her wheelchair from tipping over. There are no ramps in the curbs across from the exit to allow her access to the street and the sidewalk across the street. Wheelchair ramps need to be made.

Thank you for your time and consideration.

The letter proved to be quite effective, and the requested changes were subsequently made.

Wheelchair Condition and Maintenance

A wheelchair that is well maintained will provide reliable transportation. Power chairs are powered by batteries that need to be recharged regularly. For students who travel to and from school in their power chairs, charging can take place at home. Some students use their power chairs only at school, so their chairs remain at school and need to be charged there. It is important to develop a charging schedule and to delegate the responsibility for charging to a specific person.

Only adequately charged and properly functioning chairs should be taken into the community. There is nothing worse than having a wheelchair stop running in the middle of a community travel lesson. Power chairs can weigh anywhere from 100 to 300 pounds alone. Add to that the weight of a person, even a child, sitting in the chair, and you have a significant burden. To attempt to push a chair back to school, up hill and down dale, may put you at risk of a back injury. It may be best to throw in the towel and call for help if a wheelchair breaks down.

It is important to check the position of the controller box and to adjust it if necessary. Controller boxes, which are usually positioned on the outside of the right or left armrest, can work loose and slide out

Environmental adaptations can significantly enhance the safety of the environment for wheelchair users. Here painted stripes enhance the visibility of hazards. These adaptations were made at the request of the O&M instructor.

of position. Because of their vulnerable positioning, in many cases, they may get knocked out of position if the student has a collision on the controller side. If the controller is too near, too far away, or tipped to the right or left, the student's ability to handle the chair precisely will be diminished, and the result may be poor speed and turning control or jerking movement. If a student demonstrates these characteristics in driving it may be because the controller box needs to be adjusted. Some controller boxes are attached to flexible metal arms that are infinitely adjustable. These should be adjusted and then secured in place. If the threads that hold the controller in place become stripped, they should be replaced. However, this is often easier said than done. An alternative is to tape the box in place using heavy-duty fabric tape that comes in a variety of attractive colors and is available at hardware stores.

Conducting Transfers

At times, it may be necessary for the O&M specialist to assist the student with a transfer, either from one wheelchair to another or from a wheelchair to a stationary chair. For example, some students receive instruction in both power and manual chairs if they use them interchangeably. If the student is in the power chair when it is time for the manual chair lesson and no custodial aide is present, the O&M specialist may have to transfer the student.

No one should assist with a transfer without the proper training from an occupational or physical therapist. (The therapists that work for your school district can probably give your training if you need it.) Even with proper training, back injuries can occur, so it is also a good idea to wear a back brace during transfers. Students grow and some students present unique challenges, so transfers should be tailored and retooled to students as they grow. If a transfer does not feel right, consult with the student's physical therapist. One classroom teacher who works with orthopedically handicapped students uses this guideline for transferring students: up to 40 pounds, one person conducts the transfer; from 40 to 100 pounds, 2 people; over 100 pounds, 3 people.

Driving Etiquette

Under ideal conditions, a student will follow the etiquette of safe driving so as not to injure others (see the safety guidelines presented in Figure 8.1). It is important to teach students to take responsibility for the safety of those around them. In many cases, issues of driving etiquette become major IEP goals; for example, "John will demonstrate safe driving practices to protect pedestrians." Specific objectives under this goal might include "John will stop for pedestrians," and "John will use his horn prior to backing up."

Students with paralysis or spinal fusion may find it difficult or impossible to turn their heads to scan or look behind them. This inability creates problems when it comes to backing up or turning because they cannot see people behind them and is especially dangerous if they are in power chairs. As a rule, students should not travel backward because it is like driving a silent car blindfolded. If people are standing behind the chair with their backs turned, they will be unaware of its approach. Sometimes, however, it is necessary to back up while executing a turn or to get out of tight quarters. In such cases, the student should use the horn on the chair, if it has one, or announce in an audible voice "I'm backing up." Students should also proclaim their intentions of turning.

Students should be taught to deal with blind corners with the utmost caution, by pulling up to a corner and looking around it to see if it is clear or by traveling at a snail's pace until they are sure that it is safe to resume a normal speed. Traveling in different crowd densities presents challenges to the student in a wheelchair. Sometimes proceeding with caution at a slow pace and using the horn or saying "Excuse me" suffices. However, when it is too crowded or if the student is blind and is counting on object perception and feedback from curb detectors, it may be better to wait until the crowd has passed or to use a human guide. In such situations, the attendant can push the student in a manual chair or operate the controller of a power chair.

Travel in the Community

The community presents many immutable environmental challenges to safety for a visually impaired student in a wheelchair, including potholes, cracks in sidewalks, obscure drop-offs, curbs, and irregularities of terrain. Many students require vigilant monitoring once they leave a safe, known environment to venture out on trips into the community. Momentary lapses of attention by the teacher, the O&M specialist, aide, or attendant can result in a tipped chair. In a risky situation or on a long trip when the student tires, the O&M specialist, teacher, or aide may decide to take over operation of the controller.

If a student uses the bus to travel into the community, strict safety procedures should be followed. Once the wheelchair is loaded onto the lift, the wheelchair power should be switched off and the brakes applied. Only then should the lift be operated. Freak situations can occur, as in this example:

> In one instance, a student was safely loaded onto a lift, which carried the student up. While the student was still on the lift, the brakes on the chair were released, so that the student could travel forward into the bus. Just then, a loudly wailing fire truck roared by. The startled student inadvertently *backed* his chair up instead of going forward, just as the bus driver mistakenly lowered the guard on the edge of the lift behind the chair. The teacher yelled "Stop!" and held the chair in place. Remarkably, disaster was averted with no injury!

Wheelchair Miscellany

Motivation

Visually impaired students in manual chairs who have been pushed for years, either from necessity, expedience, or overprotection, may tend to be passive and may have undeveloped orientation abilities. Travel has "happened" to them, and they have never analyzed its whys and wherefores or had the opportunity to put themselves into action.

When challenged to become more self-directed, students find the environment more interesting and meaningful. Even if students cannot propel themselves, they may learn to deliver directions to an attendant regarding how to get somewhere. They will also experience empowerment when they can direct another to help them fulfill goals. Similarly, students who have had to give up using their power chairs to use manual chairs, for whatever reason, may retain and increase their orientation skills if they are encouraged to deliver directions to an attendant as though their voice was the controller and the attendant was the motor.

Students will be motivated to travel or direct their attendants when given choices among desirable places to go, such as a Mexican restaurant for lunch or a trip to K-Mart to buy a CD. Along the way, they should be encouraged to make all the decisions, such as those regarding street-crossing procedures and finding the best access to a street that has no wheelchair ramps. Encouraging this type of initiative stimulates students to use their vision and to develop problem-solving skills.

Shopping

When shopping in a supermarket, some students benefit from using a *shopping tray,* which is a shopping basket mounted on a small plexiglass tray that attaches to the chair over the student's lap. Students with sufficient hand and arm control may pull items from shelves and bins, place them in the basket, and transport them to a checkout stand. At the checkout stand, students who lack the dexterity to handle money should be taught to watch the entire transaction after they have relinquished their wallets to the clerk. Even if they cannot see the exact amount of the money or if they lack the math skills to calculate the transaction, they will project the impression of attentiveness and will be less likely to be purposely shortchanged. Students should also learn to solicit aid from the clerk in loading their purchases into a backpack on the back of the wheelchair.

Elevators

When traveling in shopping malls and department stores or using rapid transit, students in wheelchairs need to use elevators. Getting into and out of a crowded elevator can be difficult. Students should learn to back into the elevator after they determine that it is clear and give a warning. They will then be in a position to drive out without having to conduct turning maneuvers within a confined space.

Field Trips

At times, students are required to go on field trips to unfamiliar places. It is a good idea for the O&M specialist to make a reconnaissance trip to determine accessibility and, if necessary, to plan alternate routes from those the class will be taking.

Assessing Wheelchair Use

To set accurate goals for the O&M instruction of a student in a wheelchair and to establish a baseline from which to monitor progress, it is necessary to conduct an initial assessment of a student's wheelchair use. The Assessment for Students with Low Vision in Wheelchairs, shown in Appendix 8.A at the end of this chapter, may be used for visually impaired students in power and/or manual chairs, and parts of it may be used with students who are totally blind.

Ongoing assessment and monitoring of progress may be performed using the Community O&M Assessment and Point Chart form presented in Figure 8.2. This form may also be used in another way to record points for students who are motivated by token economies (see Chapter 5). Points may be entered as checks or tally marks each time the skill is demonstrated.

Working with students in wheelchairs can be an interesting and rewarding venture. Keeping an open, questioning, and creative attitude, tempered by a concern for safety, can yield positive results for both the O&M specialist and students.

STUDENTS WITH COMMUNICATION DISORDERS

O&M specialists are sometimes called on to serve students who have communication disorders in addition to visual impairments. Such disorders can be related to expressive or receptive language. Students may have difficulty processing spoken language and/or producing it. Some students may be able to process spoken language but be unable to speak because of brain damage. Still others may have impaired communication abilities because of deaf-blindness. Alternative means of communication, such as sign language, symbol and object communication systems, and electronic communication systems, are possible for all such students.

When working with these students, O&M specialists are advised to consult with the students' speech therapist or augmentative communication specialist. They should also work closely with the classroom teacher regarding practical details related to the students' communication systems and to provide input on O&M issues associated with communication. It is helpful for O&M specialists to learn sign language so they can use it with students who are deaf-blind and others who use it owing to expressive language disabilities. They should also become thoroughly versed in the communication systems their students use. The following sections discuss some communication systems that are used by people with communication disorders.

COMMUNITY O&M ASSESSMENT AND POINT CHART
FOR WHEELCHAIR USERS

Key to Ratings: + = Has Skill; − = Lacks Skill; E = Emerging Skill; NE = Not Evaluated at this time; NA = Not Applicable

Student _____   O&M Specialist _____

Activity	Date of Assessment				
GENERAL O&M SKILLS					
Follows directions					
Identifies landmarks					
Retains orientation					
Solicits aid					
Negotiates obstacles					
Stays to the right					
Pedestrians/crowds					
Announces back up/turns					
Stops to talk to the attendant					
Slows/stops at blind corners					
STREET CROSSINGS					
Locates wheelchair ramp or driveway					
Goes down/up middle of ramp or driveway					
Stops at bottom					
Moves out to look around obstacles					
Scans					
Locates cars					
Determines safety/danger					
Crosses when safe					
STORES/BUSINESSES					
Locates entrance					
Locates department					
Locates item					
Locates the checkout stand					
Proceeds through the line					
Communicates with clerks					
Pays					
Watches the transaction					
Locates the exit					
DANGEROUS/INAPPROPRIATE BEHAVIORS (specify)					
(Minus Points)					
_____					
_____					
_____					
_____					

FIGURE 8.2 **Sample O&M Assessment Chart for Wheelchair Users**

Tangible Symbols

Some students benefit from using *symbols* and *symbol cards* to communicate their needs. Symbols used for communication are actual objects used to represent people, places, things, or activities, while symbol cards are individual cards that present a symbolic image or images. Multiple or single images may be arranged on a card depending on a student's needs and abilities. These images may be tactile or visual according to the student's degree of visual impairment.

Regardless of the medium, the symbols must be simple and readily distinguishable to the student. If they are visual, they should be in maximum contrast and of a size commensurate with the student's visual needs. If a student who is blind is using tactile symbols, the symbols should all be labeled in print, so that those who do not know the student's system may understand what is being communicated. If the student is a braille user, the communication cards should be labeled in both print and braille.

Students can use symbol cards to make choices and to communicate them to cashiers in fast-food restaurants. If a student decides that he or she wants a hamburger, french fries, and a Coke, the student may either point to the separate symbols on a card that contains a variety of symbols that represent different menu items or present individual cards to the cashier. Students may also compose shopping lists by assembling cards with pictures of the items they want to buy. Such cards can be constructed using distinctive portions of packaging or actual pictures of the items. They may be carried in a small photo album or binder in a fanny pack, purse, pocket, or backpack.

Object Cuing

Object cuing involves the use of objects that are associated with people, places, things, or activities to represent them. For example, a Cheerio glued to a card symbolizes "breakfast." When this card is handed to the student, it can mean "It is time for breakfast. Go to the snack table."

The objects used in object cuing can be actual objects, fragments of objects, or symbolic objects. Such objects can be used in a manner that allows the student to anticipate destinations and activities or changes in destinations and activities. This feature of object cuing is particularly useful for mobility concerns and to stimulate motivation. Students may be presented with objects that signal the next destination or activity. They can also be given the opportunity to make choices from representative objects to select a favored destination. The following example shows how an object cuing symbol worked with one boy who was deaf-blind to teach him to anticipate his destinations:

> Miele, a young boy who is deaf-blind, is met by his teacher at the bus at the beginning of the school day. The teacher presents him with the symbolic object of a swatch of fake fur, chosen because the student liked to touch it, glued to a card that is attached to a cord so that it can be worn around his neck, so his hands will be free to operate his walker. Similar swatches are glued to the door frames of his two classroom doors. The swatch represents his classroom and gives him a tactile message that he is going to class. When he reaches the classroom door, the teacher coactively touches the swatch on the necklace and then the swatch on the door with him to signal that he has reached his destination. She then takes the swatch necklace from him and presents him with another necklace upon which is glued a Cheerio representing breakfast, the next activity. Embedded in this symbol is the location of the activity, the snack table. Miele examines the symbol card. The teacher puts the new card around his neck, and he proceeds with his walker to the snack table.

Using object cuing helped Miele learn to anticipate and sequence activities and to associate the objects symbolically with routes. Miele has an array of object necklaces and similar object cards from which to make choices. Initially, he performed his route from the bus to the classroom with his O&M specialist. Then the skills he was working on were supported by a designated classroom aide who had been trained by the O&M specialist. The classroom teacher and the O&M specialist worked together to isolate objects for designated destinations, and a team effort was mounted to provide repetition and consistency in practicing the routes.

Symbolic objects may be stored in what are called *anticipation* or *calendar boxes*. These devices can consist of boxes that contain several compartments, a series of boxes attached to each other, or even partitioned shelves. The idea is to allow objects to be placed in the compartments in a sequence to represent a student's schedule for a particular day. When a student is given choices, the objects may be presented in segmented *choice boxes* with two or more compartments. (For more information on tangible symbols and object cuing, see Rowland & Schweigert, 2000.)

Message Cards

Message cards are cards that display a brief written message that the student uses to communicate his or her needs to someone. They may also be used singly or in a series to prompt the student regarding an activity or sequence of activities. Sometimes students who are capable of communicating within specified situations and with informed prompting from the team need to travel in situations in which their communication abilities are taxed or insufficient for dealing with the uninformed, albeit well-intentioned, public. In such situations using *printed message cards* may be helpful.

> John, a young man in a transition program who could talk but had difficulty with memory and concentration, used a message card to communicate his destination to a bus driver. Using the card made it possible for one person to monitor his boarding the bus at one stop and another person to receive him at his destination. He was able to take responsibility for communicating his needs to the bus driver and to travel alone on the bus with the sign as a reminder to the bus driver.

> *   *   *   *   *

> Faith, a student who was both blind and mute, traveled independently around her school and used sign language to communicate with the team. However, with discouraging frequency, she turned up "lost" in the office with some anxious parent who wanted to know where the "poor little blind girl" belonged. It turned out that concerned observers had been "helping" her. People did not understand her sign language, so she was unable to refuse aid or to communicate her ability. These "helpers" disrupted her travel, causing her to become disoriented. The problem was solved, to her and everyone else's satisfaction, through the use of message cards on necklaces, one for each route, which proclaimed, for example, "I am going from the bus to Room 22. PLEASE DON'T HELP ME UNLESS I AM REALLY LOST." When accosted by a "helper," Faith pointed to or lifted up the message that hung around her neck.

Students who can read but otherwise lack sufficient communication abilities may use printed message cards with the public. Message

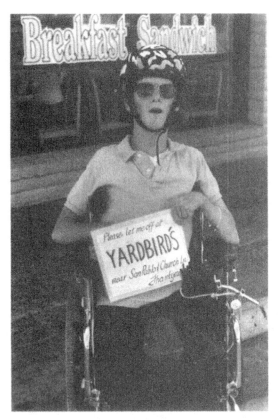

Message cards can be used in a number of situations. Here, a message card helps a student with multiple disabilities communicate his destination to a bus driver so that he can travel independently by bus.

This girl, who cannot speak, uses a message card to explain her purposeful travel and prevent well-intentioned helpers from distracting her from her route.

cards may also be used as *self-prompters* if a student has difficulty sequencing segments of a route, especially in community travel. Numbered individual cards stating each segment or step of a route or procedure may be attached in sequence on a metal ring or inserted in a small ring binder. The student may then follow the instructions step by step by turning to each successive card to read what to do next. It is also possible to use a sequence of photographs of major landmarks along a route. This technique may work well for students who cannot read but are able to recognize photographs of familiar objects or scenes.

Electronic Communication Systems

Electronic communication systems include a variety of small computers that allow the user to communicate in a variety of formats, such as simulated speech, visual output such as print, tactile output in the form of braille, or symbols on an LED display. The individual operates these devices by touching the appropriate keys to make the computer "speak" a specific word or message or to spell out words. These systems are introduced and facilitated by augmentative communication specialists. The O&M specialist may confer with this professional regarding appropriate words and messages to program into the system so the student can communicate about orientation and mobility issues.

A chapter such as this can only begin to touch on the complex subject of teaching O&M techniques to students who have multiple disabilities. Included here are some general suggestions, issues, and situations that seem to come up frequently with student teachers and ideas I have found most useful. As readers work with students who have a variety of disabilities, they will undoubtedly have many additional suggestions to add to the ones presented here.

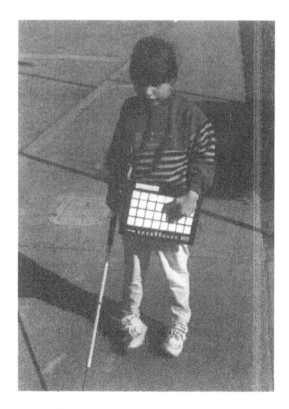

This electronic communication device allows the student to choose from a menu of different messages—such as "Hi, my name is Faith," "What is your name," "I'm hungry," "Is it safe to cross?" or "It's noisy. Will you tell me when it's safe?"—that the speech simulator can "speak" for her when she presses the appropriate button.

Orientation and Mobility Assessment
for Students with Low Vision in Wheelchairs

Name _____ Date of Birth _____ Assessor _____

Key to Ratings: + = Has Skill; − = Lacks Skill; E= Emerging Skill; NE= Not Evaluated at this time; NA= Not Applicable

	Power Chair			Manual Chair		
Activity Description	*Date*	*Rating*	*Comments*	*Date*	*Rating*	*Comments*
ATTENDANT SKILLS						
Solicits aid:						
for transfers						
for doors						
miscellaneous						
Positions chair for transfer:						
visually						
tactilely						
directs transfer						
participates in transfer						
CHAIR ETIQUETTE AND SAFETY						
Safety adaptations/use:						
helmet						
foot bracing						
horn						
hill stoppers						
curb detectors						
speed-limiting device						

Activity Description	Power Chair			Manual Chair		
	Date	Rating	Comments	Date	Rating	Comments
Uses speed appropriately						
Detects pedestrians						
distance						
Stops for pedestrians						
Slows for pedestrians						
Goes around pedestrians						
Travels with flow of pedestrians						
Verbalizes need to pass/uses horn						
Verbalizes need to back up/uses horn						
LINE OF TRAVEL						
Corresponds to line of direction:						
straight						
wavering pattern						
Needs visual clues						
constant shoreline						
other						
OBSTACLES/DROP-OFFS						
Detects obstacles						
types and distances						
Fails to detect obstacles						
types						
Negotiates obstacles						
forward						
backing						

Appendix 8.A. Orientation and Mobility Assessment *(continued)*

Activity Description	Power Chair			Manual Chair		
	Date	Rating	Comments	Date	Rating	Comments
Detects drop-offs						
types and distances						
Fails to detect drop-offs						
types						
TRAILING						
Vertical surface						
visually						
tactilely						
with curb detectors						
Takes line of direction						
Crosses open space						
Trails shoreline						
visually						
tactilely						
DOORWAYS, THRESHOLDS						
Preparation						
centered approach						
detects ramp, threshold						
changes speed as appropriate						
uses hill stoppers						
Clears frame of door						
visually						
tactilely						
with curb detectors						
Readjusts speed						

Activity Description	Power Chair			Manual Chair		
	Date	Rating	Comments	Date	Rating	Comments
TURNS						
Quarter turn (90 degree), right and left						
tactile (against wall)						
using guideline						
in free space						
About face (180 degree), right and left						
tactile (against wall)						
using guideline						
in free space						
RAMPS AND GRADES						
Up						
Adjusts speed						
Readjusts speed at top						
Applies hill stoppers						
Down						
Uses reverse to brake						
Stop-and-go technique						
Overall control						
Slows chair manually						
HEAD POSITION/SCANNING						
Positions head to maximize vision						
Holds head upright						
Scans						
Uses scan-and-go technique						
(with poor head control)						
STREET CROSSINGS						
Detects curb drop-off						

Appendix 8.A. Orientation and Mobility Assessment *(continued)*

Activity Description	Power Chair			Manual Chair		
	Date	Rating	Comments	Date	Rating	Comments
uses visual clues, such as						
crosswalk						
painted curbing						
Locates down ramps						
Locates down driveways						
Centers on ramp/driveway						
Scans at top of ramp/driveway						
Scans at bottom of ramp/driveway						
Moves out to scan around obstacles/						
parked vehicle						
Locates up ramp/driveway after						
crossing						
Centers on up ramp/driveway						

Professional
and Strategic Issues

This chapter addresses a variety of topics that may be considered professional issues—those that arise because of the nature of the O&M specialist's work. The unique situation of the O&M specialist creates some special circumstances that need to be addressed. Traveling out in the field, an O&M specialist must be prepared for many contingencies and expect the unexpected. This chapter suggests a number of ways of staying one step ahead. The first set of considerations are the legal ramifications of teaching O&M and traveling with students outside the school and in the community. Other issues involving the O&M specialist's safety include establishing and maintaining physical and mental well-being, maintaining professional boundaries, and setting limits on involvement. Next, suggestions for working effectively and harmoniously with students' support teams are discussed. Finally, as a professional—particularly one who is not always in close contact with colleagues—an O&M specialist needs to have strategies to maintain a level of involvement in the field and keep up with new developments to ensure his or her continuing effectiveness.

LEGAL AND SAFETY ISSUES

Liability

Risk is inherent to all aspects of human mobility. When a person is visually impaired or blind, with or without additional disabilities, these other factors compound the risk. For students to learn appropriate skills to fulfill their life potentials, they need to be exposed to environments and circumstances that may be risky for them. It is not surprising, then, that concerns regarding potential liability—or legal responsibility—attend the provision of O&M services.

The O&M specialist is in an acutely responsible position when evaluating students, planning for and delivering lessons, and dealing with advancement and closure issues with students. There may be potential risks in any environment, and, unlike classroom teachers, O&M specialists can exercise only a limited degree of control over their teaching environments. They need to be concerned with protecting themselves against any possible claims of negligence in the event of accidents or injuries to their students. Such protection involves meticulous planning and foresight; avoidance of unnecessarily risky situations, particularly transporting students in private cars; and protecting oneself legally as much as possible through use of permission forms (see Chapter 2) and professional liability insurance.

It is difficult to make blanket statements about liability, especially about professional insurance, because situations vary from place to place. However, Marsh, Hartmeister, and Griffin-Shirley (2000) addressed at length the legal issues facing O&M specialists. They suggested a number of strategies for reducing the risks of liability that are important to consider and to put into practice (see Sidebar 9.1). The most important point about liability, however, as summarized in their conclusion is worth repeating:

> Consider how to do the best job professionally for students, not how to avoid liability. Seek to attain a balance between the maximum benefits of O&M training for students and minimal risks to their safety. Always attempt to minimize risks, not only for self-protection, but for the protection of the students (p. 507).

Keeping Safe as a Teacher

As was discussed earlier in this book (see Chapter 5), safety concerns have to be part of every O&M lesson. It is important, however, for O&M specialists—especially those who are itinerant or home based—to be mindful of safety considerations not only to protect their students, but to maintain their own well-being. The following guidelines are based on direct experience (derived, in part, from guidelines pro-

Strategies for Minimizing the Risks of Liability

Goals and Instruction

* Have clearly written goals that include every skill that will be taught. Teach only new skills that are in the controlling objectives, so students and their parents or guardians cannot claim that they did not understand the risks or did not approve the instruction.

* Use lesson plans and keep anecdotal records that describe what occurred during all lessons, including the skills that were covered and the performance levels the student attained.

* Avoid making promises about the level of attainment or the time span in which O&M goals will be achieved.

* When a concept is integral to instruction of a new skill, ensure that the student comprehends it by teaching the concept first, especially to a child and to a person with limited cognitive abilities. From a negligence-based perspective, do not teach a concept or O&M skills that are dependent on the concept that are beyond the student's ability to understand and to demonstrate independently.

* Avoid conducting lessons outdoors in inclement weather if the student is medically fragile.

* Investigate instructional sites beforehand to determine whether possible risks are present. If there is no time to visit a new site before a lesson, spend ample time analyzing the site with the student prior to the lesson and model appropriate problem-solving behavior.

* Be prepared for emergencies. For example, carry a cellular telephone to call for help and a basic first-aid kit.

Disclosure and Documentation

* Have students and parents or guardians of minors sign disclosure forms that explain the risks inherent in the various aspects of O&M training. Before a new area of instruction is begun, explain the risks involved and have the appropriate persons sign the amended disclosure forms that describe these risks.

* Document safety concerns and the fact that all students and their parents or guardians have been apprised of these concerns and notify officials, rehabilitation counselors, or parents or guardians in writing of these concerns. Include such issues as the disclosure of medical conditions, need for medications, and students' responsibility for personal care.

* Resolutely respect the confidentiality of students.

Assessment

* Assess all students who are assigned and conduct ongoing assessments of students in the caseload. If O&M instruction or instruction in a particular skill or activity is not deemed appropriate for a student, clearly state the reasons for this conclusion in the assessment report.

Sidebar 9.1 Strategies for Minimizing the Risks of Liability *(continued)*

- When terminating a student's O&M instruction, clearly state the level of proficiency the student acquired and the reasons for discontinuing instruction. In the final report, also clearly describe any skill areas in which the student has not attained a satisfactory level of proficiency and state that the student has been told of these deficiencies and how they may affect safe travel.

- If a student is uncooperative to the point that his or her safety is at risk, have a colleague observe several lessons and document the student's behavior. Report the behavior in writing to the proper authorities or supervisors (such as the school or agency director) and ask for advice. If the behavior continues, hold a meeting of the student's educational or rehabilitation team in which the problem and what has been done or can be done to alleviate it are discussed.

Training and Supervision

- Make sure that any teacher or rehabilitation aide who will monitor a student's O&M skills is adequately trained to do so.

- Maintain professional certification through the Academy for the Certification of Vision Education and Rehabilitation Professionals.

- Stay familiar with the professional literature and attend conferences regularly to remain up to date with the newest information in the O&M field.

Transportation

- Avoid transporting students in a private car. Instead ask family members to transport the students; use public transportation, such as buses, taxis, or subways, when feasible; or arrange for students to be transported by school-district buses.

- If students must be transported in a private car, observe the following precautions: (1) carry the maximum amount of automobile liability insurance allowed in the state, (2) designate the car for business use, (3) obtain annual written permission from parents or guardians for students to ride in the car, (4) observe all motor vehicle laws, (5) take a defensive driving course, (6) ensure that the car is well maintained and keep records of all maintenance and repairs, and (7) make sure that the car is equipped with dual air bags and that it has a switch that can deactivate the passenger-side air bag when a young child is being transported.

Exposure to Liability

- Be familiar with and follow the tenets of federal and state laws that affect the O&M profession.

- Verify to what extent, if any, statutory provisions of immunity in a given jurisdiction may reduce or eliminate the risk of personal liability for negligent acts.

- Talk to a knowledgeable representative of the employing agency or school district about the applicability of the agency's or district's insurance coverage and obtain written verification of coverage in all insurance policies. Check periodically to determine if this insurance coverage has changed and record all discussions in writing.

- If the employing agency or school district does not provide liability-based insurance protection, persuade the agency or district to provide individual, personal coverage and coverage for transporting students in a personal car, if appropriate.
- Consider purchasing the maximum amount of liability insurance through a professional association or union.
- When possible, use mobility tools that have been purchased from a manufacturer or vendor that has thoroughly field-tested all designs and products. Although doing so does not automatically guarantee protection from potential liability, such field tests reduce the risk of equipment failure. With a self-constructed, adaptive mobility device, exposure to negligence-based liability is increased if the device fails to perform as desired and a compensable injury results.

Reprinted with permission from R. A. Marsh, F. Hartmeister, & N. Griffin-Shirley, "Legal Issues for Orientation and Mobility Specialists: Minimizing the Risks of Liability," *Journal of Visual Impairment & Blindness*, 94 (August 2000), pp. 495–507.

posed by itinerant teachers at Pupil Services and Cameron School in the West Contra Costa Unified School District in California). To some, these measures may appear extreme, but to others they will be standard practice. They reflect conservative measures that promote safety in a variety of situations.

1. Maintain your vehicle in safe operating condition.

2. Keep your vehicle's doors locked while driving.

3. Do not park in isolated areas of parking lots.

4. Keep your key ready when going to your vehicle.

5. Call in advance to new destinations to ask about safety-related issues, such as the best way to get there and where to park.

6. Plan safe routes to destinations.

7. Be sure that your posted schedule indicates a time frame and your destination and a phone number, when applicable.

8. Be sure that someone else (such as a secretary) is aware of your daily schedule and any variations that arise.

9. Take a partner to home visits in questionable neighborhoods.

10. Take a "body guard" along on night evaluations and do these evaluations in "safe" areas.

11. Avoid making home visits if there are critical family problems.

12. Inform your supervisor of all unusual conditions or problems.

13. Carry personal work-identification and emergency information with you.

14. When working alone in a classroom, lock the doors.

The reason for including carrying identification among these safety guidelines may not be immediately apparent, but occasions can arise when it is crucial to be able to prove who you are and what you are doing. O&M specialists may not realize how easily their activities can be misunderstood by passers-by or even law enforcement personnel, as the following examples show:

> On a spring afternoon, early in my teaching career, I conducted a lesson in monocular use and address systems with a tall adolescent boy. It took place in a quiet residential area. At the end of the lesson I returned the student to his school, got into my Volkswagen, and drove toward the freeway that would take me to my next site. As usual, the rear seat of my car was piled high with boxes of teaching paraphernalia.
>
> As I approached the on ramp, I realized that I was being followed by an unmarked car with a flashing red light. I immediately pulled over and rolled down my window. A tall man in a tweed jacket sauntered over, perused the contents of my backseat, pulled a badge from his jacket pocket, and announced that he was a plainclothes policeman. He then proceeded to question me minutely about my activities of the previous hour with a young man and a telescope. By one of those odd coincidences of life, the neighborhood in which we had been working recently had suffered a rash of robberies, and the officer was staked out there looking for suspects. My student and I qualified. He asked me for my driver's license and a full explanation of my activities, which I promptly gave. He also wanted some proof of my employment with the school district. At the time, I had no official job identification, but since it was during a major gasoline shortage, I had a letter from the director of Pupil Services identifying me as a person employed in the school district who could not perform my job of itinerant teaching without an adequate fuel supply. To my great relief, this letter satisfied the policeman.

In other incidents, a male O&M specialist was arrested in the course of teaching for following his female student. A female O&M

specialist who was standing on a street corner working on street crossings with her male student was attacked by a prostitute who proceeded to bludgeon her with a purse in a territorial act of aggression. Although not all such situations may be resolved simply by presenting appropriate identification, it is a good idea to carry and even to wear some form of professional identification. Some O&M specialists wear jackets with a logo reflecting their profession and/or identifying them with an agency. They may also wear identification badges.

In addition, as noted in Chapter 2, when making your initial contact with a school, it is essential to introduce yourself to the principal, school secretaries, and security personnel, as well as to other site personnel. These introductions serve two purposes. They establish your legitimate purpose in being at the school and may help to alleviate the interference of well-intentioned people who are bent on helping "lost" students. When they spy the O&M specialist in the vicinity, they will be less likely to rush to the aid of the student who is struggling toward independence.

The Hazards of Overinvolvement

One of the occupational hazards of the helping professions is *overinvolvement*. Because of the one-on-one nature of O&M instruction, the O&M specialist is at risk. It is not uncommon for students to present distressing psychological and situational needs that can become the main focus of the instructional period if they are not handled through the proper channels. For example, the O&M specialist may be drawn into lengthy "counseling" sessions with emotionally troubled students. It is important to recognize the professional limits of your occupation and to be well informed about the availability of appropriate counseling and support resources and the means of marshaling their support.

Although the primary purpose of the O&M specialist is to teach O&M skills, at times psychological and situational needs may interfere. A student may present chronic or violent tantrum behavior to such a degree that teaching is impossible. When students present chronic behavioral problems that prevent their learning or jeopardize their physical well-being or that of others, placement in a class that focuses on management and behavioral issues may be appropriate. The O&M specialist can support this option by discussing it with other team members and by documenting her experience of the student's behavior. An IEP meeting may then be convened to explore a change of placement for the student. Or, it may become evident that a student is not getting enough to eat, is suicidal, or is the object of physical or sexual abuse. The O&M specialist may have a role to play in all these situations, but it is a role limited to and by his or her professional capacities. Ideally, it is a role that balances the dedication to humane and professional standards with the recognition that taking on responsibilities that draw one from the sphere of one's primary commitment to teaching ultimately can shortchange the student and lead one into the stressful condition of overinvolvement.

During an O&M specialist's career, he or she may encounter students who are the objects of some forms of abuse—physical, sexual, or emotional. Those with disabilities are at a particular risk of abuse because of their increased vulnerability. A student may come to school with cigarette burns or extensive bruises, exhibit a syndrome of behaviors indicative of sexual abuse, or report that he or she is a victim of abuse. In some cases, it will be unclear whether abuse has actually taken place. Regardless of the clarity or degree of evidence presented, all such situations should be fully explored, following the requirements of local laws and school district regulations, with due regard for confidentiality, but with the assistance of the appropriate personnel: the principal or supervisor, possibly other teachers, the school nurse or school psychologist. Every state has enacted legislation that mandates the reporting of child abuse and neglect following the Child Abuse Prevention and Treatment Act (P.L. 104–235). Teachers and other school personnel are among the individuals designated as mandatory reporters in all states. Many states have toll-free reporting numbers, and there is a national child help number to report abuse (800-4-A-CHILD). Local child protective service agencies may need to be called, and some states require that the police be called.

WORKING WITH THE SUPPORT TEAM

The support team is composed of individuals who come into contact with the student in a variety of settings, both encompassing and transcending the immediate school environment. Thus, it includes, but goes beyond, the educational team that prepares and carries out the student's Individualized Education Program (IEP). The entire team may comprise fellow students; student aides; classroom aides; teachers and student teachers; parents, siblings, and other family members; psychologists; bus drivers; medical specialists; physical, occupational, and speech therapists; adaptive physical education teachers; custodians; secretaries; and store clerks.

The importance of a support team cannot be overstated. Ideally, each member contributes his or her knowledge, efforts, and abilities to form the fabric of a far-reaching network that upholds, augments, and nurtures the ongoing well-being and development of the student. All the potential members of a support team are present within the reaches of a student's environment. However, they may need to be recruited as conscious and united players with explicit and common goals. The IEP process is designed to accomplish this end and does so to a degree. O&M specialists can contribute to team building by enlisting other team members to support and reinforce their students' O&M instruction and by offering them training in O&M concepts and skills.

Building a Network

In most instances, an O&M specialist is only as effective as the support team on which he or she is a player, especially when the specialist is working with preschool and elementary-level students or students with multiple and/or developmental disabilities. Commonly, with these students, a consistent global approach and repetition are key elements to the promotion of their mastery of a skill. Therefore, it is most effective when all those who work with them on a daily basis emphasize and reinforce the same skills, as in the example of Marisa:

> Marisa, a preschool student who is blind, is learning to use her cane as a probe. However, when left to her own devices, she tends to let her cane gradually drift behind her, where it does no good. When all the important others in the network are united in providing intermittent, coactive physical modeling for the skill of sliding her cane "in front" along with verbal prompting for "in front," Marisa will learn to practice the behavior sooner and with greater consistency than if she were to practice it only in the presence of her O&M teacher for several half hours per week.

When they join forces to reinforce specific learning behaviors, the support team is working as a network—that is, as an interconnected system. The network effect can be created and strengthened through individual and group training and consultation sessions initiated by the O&M specialist, who remains accessible as a continuing resource for any questions or challenges that arise. Communicating educational concerns and methods through these means amplifies the effects of one-on-one instruction beyond the scheduled O&M teaching periods, thus expanding students' learning into the greater context of their daily lives. In this manner, consistency and repetition are ensured.

Training for the Support Team

Training sessions for members of support teams provide a forum for O&M specialists to introduce themselves and explain their function as teachers and their role in the networks. Training is a means of teaching that enables the team members to participate actively through hands-on learning experiences. It expands the participants' knowledge of the O&M challenges that face students who are visually impaired or blind and lends visibility and credibility to the practice of O&M instruction. Training sessions may be presented to groups, such as the faculty at a school; to smaller clusters of people who work directly with a student; or to individuals.

A common type of training, directed toward teachers, aides, and fellow students of a student who is blind or visually impaired, is designed to explain travel techniques for those with visual impairment and blindness. Such training may be presented in one or more segments, depending on the number, age, and learning abilities of the participants. Participants usually receive practical instruction in the techniques, using occluders to simulate types of visual impairment and blindness. Under the direction of the O&M specialist, participants alternately assume the role of guide and guided and practice basic skills. If teachers are creative (or have acquaintances who are), they can design a simple booklet describing and illustrating the basic techniques that are being introduced. This booklet can be given to each participant to reinforce what they have learned and for future reference.

This type of training has the greatest impact when the visually impaired student participates (assuming that participation is appropriate in terms of the student's age and abilities). Fellow students and teachers alike usually listen responsively, especially when students share information about themselves and their experiences and take questions from the audience. As stars of the show, students gain practice in developing advocacy skills and build self-esteem.

Training can also be offered one on one to individuals who have daily direct contact with a student who is visually impaired or blind.

This type of training is critical to ensuring a consistent learning environment for the student. Typically, parents, classroom teachers, and aides are targeted to receive this kind of instruction. They may be taught such things as basic skills, the rudiments of cane travel, and strategies for reinforcing the training that the O&M specialist has initiated with the student. When important others in students' environment reliably model accurate techniques and provide consistent prompting and cuing, students learn faster, and there is less of a tendency for their practice of techniques to erode and become inefficient or unsafe.

Training aides, classroom teachers, and parents to support accurate mobility skills with the student is a time-consuming and exacting process, but the returns will reveal an investment well made. It is important to monitor the work of the support team regularly to evaluate and reinforce the accuracy of the members' performance in supporting the O&M concepts and behaviors that have been taught and to determine when to alter procedures or set new goals. Monitoring can be accomplished through scheduled observations at school and home visits.

When a blind or visually impaired student's classmates are of preschool and kindergarten age, they may need to receive simplified and modified training. Children of this age have difficulty grasping and generalizing the concepts of visual impairment and blindness, especially in the sense of its permanence and wide-reaching effects. It is helpful for the O&M specialist to come back from time to time to answer questions and to allow them to use occluders and canes (with careful supervision) as a regularly available recess activity. Although students may not grasp the full implications of this play activity, they greatly enjoy pursuing it and will request it repeatedly.

For groups of young children, I have found it useful to teach a technique called "shoulder guiding" instead of regular human guide skills. In this technique, the guide stands directly in front of the guided. The guided places his or her right or left hand on the corresponding shoulder of the guide so as to establish and maintain a rearward position relative to the guide. This position guarantees advance warning of level changes, such as stairs and uneven terrain. Standing behind the guide also prevents the guide from inadvertently walking the guided into obstacles, such as desks and poles, since young human guides commonly have not yet learned to assess spatial

Although not a standard O&M technique, some instructors find that shoulder guiding works well for young children, such as these preschoolers coming in from recess, until they can learn more formal techniques.

dimensions beyond the boundaries of their own bodies. As young students mature and develop broader concepts of another's body in space and the appropriate protective strategies, they can be taught standard human guide skills. Although some O&M specialists discourage teaching this modification of a standard technique because young students may not want to give it up in favor of the human guide technique later, I have found that the safety benefits outweigh any inconvenience in retraining students.

Promoting Consistency and Involvement with the Team

There are several ways to promote consistency and accuracy when more than one person is supporting the practice of skills with the student. Sequenced checklists of target behaviors can be used, such as the Community O&M Assessment and Point Chart for Wheelchair Users in Chapter 8. Printed scripts and guidelines can also be used, such as those provided in Chapter 7 for cane travel.

It is important for each teaching team member to be involved in the O&M teaching process. Parents, and sometimes classroom teachers and long-term aides, know the student better than the O&M specialist and can provide a wealth of information to flesh out teaching strategies. It is essential to involve the important others in planning and implementing beyond the IEP meeting by holding regular consultation and brainstorming and evaluative sessions conducted in person and over the phone. (Brainstorming can be a particularly fruitful activity when conducted in a nonjudgmental atmosphere in which the participants are encouraged to toss out ideas relative to a particular teaching challenge. When wild and impractical flashes of inspiration are as welcome as their more down-to-earth and practical counterparts, truly innovative and effective strategies can be freely conceived.) Notes can also be sent back and forth between the parents and teacher, with the student, or in the student's backpack. Videos of the student's progress and accomplishments at school can be sent home for the parents to view. Using such channels of communication between the players stimulates and maintains the vitality of the network. Networking is an exciting and creative process that, when activated, fuels itself.

The support team provides direct educational support for the student. It also provides support for the team members, who may experience times of frustration and loneliness and feelings of hopelessness and impotence in the face of teaching challenges or difficult circumstances. At such times, other team members can be invited to share their knowledge and lend support and encouragement. The support team in its entirety, from children to adults, is a living resource that can transcend and increase the effectiveness of each individual involved. It thrives on good and consistent communication among conscious, informed, and united players. Sidebar 9.2 lists some suggestions for working effectively and harmoniously with other team members.

The Teacher as Communicator

To be an effective teacher, one must work at being an effective communicator. The art of communication does not always come naturally, but it may be cultivated in a conscious manner. This involves open-

---

SIDEBAR 9.2 **Tips for Teaming**

O&M specialists are members of support teams for each of their students and at a number of different schools. It can take a lot of time and effort to cultivate effective relationships with each group. Moreover, as a consequence of the itinerant nature of their job, they may sometimes have a tendency to feel isolated. The following suggestions will help O&M specialists to maintain a healthy connection with their teams:

* Keep in mind that the student is the primary team member, the hub of the team.
* Stay in touch regularly with other team members.
* Develop and sustain effective communication skills and channels.
* Keep consistent and accurate records so that you and others will have access to a factual paper trail.
* Find out what teaching strategies have already been tried and what does or does not work for a particular student.
* Let the team know what strategies are working for you.
* Keep in mind that no one has all the answers.
* Keep in mind that others may have new and different insights about the student.
* Ask questions and encourage them from other team members.
* Do not be shy about asking for help in the face of challenges.
* Work for consistent reinforcement for the student's practice of major O&M skills across all environments.

---

ing and sustaining channels of communication. What one communicates is strongly affected by how one communicates it. If, as Marshall McCluen stated, "the medium is the message," then the trappings of communication can be as important as the content. How one communicates can enhance or detract from the message one wishes to convey.

Being a team member necessitates receiving, interpreting, and imparting information. If one neglects or declines any aspect of this role, the team and students will miss out; if one declines all aspects of the role, one has chosen to exit as a player on the team. The O&M specialist's teaching position in the public schools necessitates communication with a wide variety of people who are associated in different capacities with the student, ranging from the students' peers to medical specialists. Selecting the method or combination of methods that will best communicate one's message to a particular individual or group can become a teaching technique or strategy that advances the welfare of the students and others who are involved. The following communication methods are all critical components of interactions with these individuals and represent aspects of the medium of interpersonal exchanges.

- *Face-to-face, spoken communications* with one or more individuals, including consultations, conferences, meetings, and training sessions. These encounters may be accompanied by other types of communications, such as telephone calls, notes, e-mail, or voice mail, to reinforce or follow up what has been communicated.

- *Written communications,* including print, large-print, and braille notes when other team members are visually impaired or blind, memos, letters, evaluations, or reports. Such communications are the necessary currency of the regular work in the public schools.

- *Electronic communications,* including faxes and e-mail messages. These communications may be passed to and from other professionals in the field, people at different school sites, in short, anyone who needs fast access to documents or other written information.

- *Telephone communications,* including direct one-on-one and conference calls and voice mail. These serve to help team members stay in touch and to address issues of immediate importance. Telephone calls are particularly important in communicating with parents and others who serve the student in different capacities. Conference calls may be advised at meetings at which those who are meeting are in geographically diverse locations.

- *Visual and tactile communications,* including videos, photos, drawings, raised-line drawings and other tactile means, and demonstrations. These methods have significant applications in a variety of teaching situations that include the students or parents and others who support the student.

- *Auditory communications,* including tapes. These communications may be used with students and others who may benefit from notes or information that would be difficult for them to access by other means.

- *Proxy communications* or using another professional who is versed in the concern being addressed. For example, when the O&M specialist is unable to attend a meeting, it may be necessary for another O&M specialist or the teacher of students with visual impairments to represent him or her and present certain information.

The methods of communication that are available to us as both teachers and team members are many and diverse. In each situation, it is important to consider which method will best represent and convey the message. If the intended recipient of the communication does not seem to be "getting it," then another method may be more effective. It is also helpful to bear in mind that a critical part of being a teacher is to be a learner and that all situations can present opportunities for learning. Receiving information can be as important as imparting it.

Not only the method of communication, but the manner in which it is presented, will influence how it is received. Sidebar 9.3 presents some suggestions for enhancing the effectiveness of communication in any situation. It is also important to recognize that our position as O&M specialists confers an advisory role, and this position entails the responsibility of being accurate, truthful, and diplomatic.

Effective communication is especially important in facilitating and enhancing the work of the support team. Sustaining channels of communication maintains the vitality of communication. It can be accomplished by enhancing the human bonds in the network by means such as these:

- *supporting* others in words and actions

- *encouraging* others

- *recognizing and acknowledging* the gifts and efforts of others

- *thanking* others in tangible ways through words, notes, and gifts

- *affirming* others through sensitive acts of kindness

THE TEACHER AS STUDENT

Being an effective teacher requires not only remaining informed about one's area of expertise, but maintaining the vitality of one's interest in the tasks at hand. It may be accomplished, in part, by assuming the role

SIDEBAR 9.3 **Tips for Effective Communication**

A number of factors affect the strength and effectiveness of your communication with others. Regardless of whether you are discussing a student's assessment with other professionals on a student's educational team; presenting a training session to other members of the support team such as parents and students; or talking on the telephone to a vendor of adaptive equipment, the following suggestions will increase the chances that your message is well received:

- *Make sure your message is concise and intelligible.* This involves gauging the attentiveness and comprehension level of those with whom you communicate. You may need to obtain the services of a translator, especially in culturally diverse districts.

- *Be knowledgeable about and sensitive toward the beliefs, values, attitudes and behaviors of different cultures* (see Milian & Erin, 2001).

- *Pay attention to the timing of your message.* Choose the appropriate moment and the most effective method or methods for communication. Follow up to evaluate whether the communication was received and its relevance and/or efficacy.

- *Be appropriately assertive.* Match your tone to the situation and receptiveness of those with whom you are communicating.

- *Develop and use negotiating skills.* Try to maintain a "win-win" atmosphere to promote reasonable compromises.

of the perpetual student. Teachers as students study their students, themselves, the environment, cause-and-effect relationships, and the weather, among other things. They also maintain their studies in the academic sense, keeping abreast of new developments in their field and related fields.

Asking Questions

It is important to approach one's teaching with a questioning attitude and to harness one's energies into the service of answering the endless series of questions that arise about each student: Why does this student always veer to the left? Why isn't this intervention strategy working? What can I do to facilitate monetary transactions with this student? How can I prevent a student's curb detectors from catching in the locker vents? How can I help the student to strengthen his upper body? How can I help the student to differentiate traffic patterns at a busy intersection? and so forth.

As teachers, we can fall back on the general guidelines and pre-scribed techniques retained from our formal education, but many student-specific questions just cannot be answered once and for all. It falls upon us to be insatiably curious detectives attempting to solve some of life's smaller mysteries. When we start asking questions, we are making the first step in the process of creative problem solving. Not all our answers will work. And some will work in surprising ways, as occurred with Clarissa:

> Clarissa was working on the concept of a block and travel around it starting from her house and ending at her house. Her house was on a noisy street, but the other three streets bounding the block were quiet. For some reason, Clarissa could not iden-tify when she had reached her street, despite counting corners and having the auditory clue of heavy traffic. I asked myself over and over what else I could do to help Clarissa identify her noisy street. I had made a tactile map of her neighborhood showing her street and the four houses on her block. As a last resort, I attached a strip of sandpaper to her street on the map, allowed her to examine it tactilely, and referred to it as "Barrett, the noisy or sandpaper street." The next time we traveled around the block, Clarissa was able to identify her street! Linking the tactile "noise" of the sandpaper with the auditory noise of the street solidified the identification for her.

Anecdotal Records

Keeping anecdotal records on one's students is a powerful means of studying them in the immediate present and over the long term. As noted in Chapter 3, anecdotal records are brief notes that document every con-tact with a student, including the date and time of each event, a brief description, and comments. Anecdotal records may consist of brief state-ments about the content of a lesson, the destination of a route, and the student's performance, such as how many safe crossings he or she accom-plished, including any progress made or problems that arise. Such records will help one in lesson planning, isolating problem areas, prob-lem solving, establishing goals and monitoring progress. This informa-tion can be recorded on a simple form, such as the one the O&M special-ist used to record Jeremy's activities in the example given in Figure 9.1. O&M specialists may find it helpful to jot notes on 3x5-inch cards during a lesson for future reference or to be converted later to anecdotal records.

ANECDOTAL RECORD

Student _Jeremy Jenson_   **O&M Specialist** _Knott_

Date/time	Comments
1/15 (1 hr.) 4/4 crossings safe	_Trip To McKay's Market._ J. alert and brisk today. Responsive to prompts for technique. Good safe independent crossings—all 4! First time! Worked on concept of IN FRONT and BESIDE streets, and naming them (Mason, Market, etc.). He knew he did well today. At the market, J. worked on locating Fig Newtons and differentiating packages. Independent purchase. _GOOD DAY!_
1/18 (1 hr.) 3/4 crossings safe	_School community._ J. very slow and "tired" today. Many stops. Worked on crossings, emphasizing IN FRONT, BESIDE streets and their names. Also appropriate place to "park" cane prior to scanning at crossings.
1/22	J. absent.
1/24 (1.5 hrs.)	_Field trip with class to MacDonald's._ O&M lesson during trip. Emphases: controlling and storing cane, stairs, and fares on bus. J. appears a lot more blind in an unknown environment.
1/29 (1 hr.) 3/4 crossings safe	_Trip To McKay's._ J. still requires some prompts at crossings for (1) Alignment to appropriate street at Mason, (2) pace. Worked on concept of second stop and scan around an obstacle (truck parked at curb). At McKay's, couldn't locate juice without prompt for initial turn. Purchase fully independent but couldn't remember the cost of the item. Worked on stairs. Up very good with prompt only on measurement. Still working on alignment at top.
1/31 (1 hr.) 4/4 crossings safe	_School community._ We used the tape recorder today to make an auditory map of the route. This was reinforcing and highly motivating. Emphasized identity and names and positions of the streets; walking in step—difficult but emerging.

FIGURE 9.1 **Example of an Anecdotal Record for an O&M Student**

The simple act of writing anecdotal records can provide a fruitful time for focusing on a lesson that has transpired to consider what training approaches have worked well and what might be improved, changed, or adapted to the student. Anecdotal records may also contain any other significant information that arises concerning the student and interactions with important others. They also document dates and amounts of time spent on lessons.

Self-Study

Turning an appraising eye upon oneself may not always be comfortable but it has its rewards. Taking a few steps back and questioning the effectiveness of one's teaching methods and delivery can help an O&M specialist to grow. Using a tape recorder to tape lessons may be illuminating, as is having one's lessons videotaped. Such means can help to answer the following questions: Am I targeting and hitting the essentials? Am I giving too much or too little instruction? Am I adequately supportive? What is the student's response? It is also good to be receptive to any suggestions that peers suggest or supervisors make when doing their regular evaluations of one's performance.

Retooling

O&M specialists can keep themselves primed for teaching by keeping abreast of current literature in the field, attending seminars and conferences, and taking courses. Continuing education is a means by which they may remain current with developments in the field and grow in other areas of knowledge. O&M specialists can expand their areas of expertise by earning credentials in other fields. Conferences and consultations with other professionals can help them to gain knowledge. Maintaining active memberships in professional organizations and subscribing to professional journals helps them stay connected and informed. Networking with other O&M specialists, at meetings, conferences, and via email or the telephone, provides support, inspiration, and assistance with problem solving. When an O&M specialist is in an isolated area and has no immediate or direct contact with peers in the field, he or she may connect with other O&M specialists via a variety of O&M sites on the Internet (see the Resources section for some examples).

THE WELL-EQUIPPED TEACHER

As itinerant professionals, O&M specialists need to plan ahead. They are always moving from school to school and place to place and cannot count on opening a desk drawer or closet to find just what they need. To meet the exigencies of the moment, they need to have a number of items close at hand. The car trunk and glove compartment are excellent storage places because the car, for an itinerant teacher, is a mobile office and, at times, classroom that goes wherever he or she goes.

Staple items in this mobile office may be organized in file boxes, in plastic bins of various sizes, and in zipper-style plastic bags. The items listed in Sidebar 9.4 are those I have found particularly useful or desirable. This list is not exhaustive because of the enormous variety of materials and teaching situations that arise, and it does not include many other essential teaching aids that an O&M specialist will also need to fulfill the needs of specific teaching situations. As you work with your students, you will undoubtedly come up with a list of staple items that will reflect their needs. Some items may be retired from the list and others added as they become necessary.

SIDEBAR 9.4 **Checklist for the Mobile Office**

The following items may be considered the minimum for a well-equipped O&M specialist. Although it is not an exhaustive list, each O&M specialist will find items that need to be added and subtracted in the course of his or her own professional experience and depending on his or her particular students.

- *Critical information* for each student. This information includes all vital names, addresses, phones, emergency procedures, and release forms to obtain medical treatment.
- *Professional teacher information.* This information includes some proof of employment in the form of an identification badge, card, or letter proving employment by the school district.
- *File for professional and record-keeping forms.* It is a great convenience and time saver to have every form that you may need at your fingertips.
- *Pager and/or cellular telephone.* It is a good idea to have these items if your professional or personal budget allows to save time, to increase accessibility, and to use in urgent and emergency situations.

Sidebar 9.4 Checklist for the Mobile Office *(continued)*

- *Change for telephone calls.* It is a good idea to have a constant reserve of coins in case you need to make an urgent call from a pay telephone in the event that you do not have a cell phone or it does not function in the particular location where you happen to be.

- *Maps* of all areas where you may be traveling and of the schools that you frequent. These maps help in lesson planning and in keeping you oriented.

- *Current transit schedules and maps and transit company phone numbers.* These schedules and numbers are helpful if a bus is missed or if there are any other problems that arise in association with public transit.

- *First aid kit,* including disposable rubber gloves and a sugar source, such as Reactose, for diabetic students. It is always possible for a student to sustain a minor injury, such as a skinned knee, during an O&M lesson.

- *Moist towelettes.* Moist towelettes help with the inevitable cleanups, especially of dirty hands.

- *Facial tissues.* Tissues are necessary for dealing with colds and allergies.

- *Sun screen.* The accumulated years in the sun can take their toll. It is best to protect yourself and avoid the risk of skin cancer.

- *Visors, visored caps, hats (including safari hats).* This headgear is good for personal use or for students who, for one reason or another, do not have their own.

- *Monoculars, magnifiers, sunglasses.* It is good to have a collection of samples for students to try out in the field to help them make the most practical and personalized selection. The information gleaned from such trials can be conveyed to parents and eye care specialists who will make the ultimate decisions regarding a student's acquisition of aids. It is also good to have a stock of these items for use in case a student forgets or loses his or her own. Sunglasses with broad-spectrum protection are an excellent aid for the teacher, both while driving and conducting outdoor lessons.

- *Lens cleaner and lens tissues.* Students invariably get fingerprints on lenses, regardless of admonitions. Since body oils are acidic and over time will etch glass and plastic, it is a good idea to have students clean lenses (of eyeglasses and other optical aids) when necessary to maintain the best optical quality.

- *Spare canes in several sizes.* Spare canes are needed to substitute for a student's misplaced or broken cane.

- *Cane tips.* Cane tips can break, wear out, and fall off. If you have a collection of tips for all the types of canes that students use, replacing them is a simple, expedient matter.

- *Measuring tape.* A measuring tape is needed for sizing canes "on the spot."

- *Steel wool, alcohol and cotton, wax, or bar soap.* These items are helpful for cleaning and conditioning recalcitrant joints on folding canes.

- *Red reflective tape.* The reflective tape on white canes can become rapidly worn and often needs to be replaced.

- *Heavy-duty fabric tape.* This tape is excellent for reinforcing cane tips and curb detectors and for taping speed-control switches on wheelchairs or securing controllers when necessary.

- *Fanny packs and backpacks.* When students do not have their own fanny packs or backpacks or forget them, spare ones are an invaluable aid to shopping. Wearing one in front is good for storing and handling a shopping list and money. You may also need a fanny pack or backpack to transport materials and aids in the field and to keep your hands free for tactile interventions and prompts.

- *Tape recorder and blank tapes.* These items are useful for taping lessons for motivating a student and for self-study.

- *Poncho.* Students sometimes come without adequate rain gear. A poncho will do in a pinch.

- *Waterproof headgear* that does not cover the ears. Such headgear ensures unobstructed hearing in wet weather.

- *Two umbrellas.* Keep one for you and a spare for a student who has forgotten his or her own.

- *Rubber shoes or boots* for you. They are essential in wet weather.

- *Cane gloves or gloves without fingers.* Keep a pair of such gloves in a universal size for cane users to borrow in frigid weather if they do not have their own.

- *A tactile diagram kit* such as a Chang Kit, Picture Maker, the Wheatley Tactile Diagraming Kit, or teacher-made concept kits.

- *Felt-tip pens* in black and colors, *heavy-duty drawing paper, Quick-Draw paper or raised-line drawing paper, Wikki-Stix, and Dri-Erase Board.* These items can be used to create on-the-spot visuals, "tactiles," and maps for learning moments and to reinforce the teaching of concepts in general.

- *Large-print and braille compasses.* These compasses help with teaching and establishing cardinal directions.

- *Tote bags, plastic bags, heavy-duty shopping bags with handles, wheeled luggage, or collapsible carts.* These can be used to carry all the other teaching paraphernalia that you use from your car to the class and back. It is a good idea to have plastic bags for rainy weather.

- *Walkie-talkies.* Walkie-talkies are useful for keeping in touch with advanced travelers who are within a two-mile range, as when you follow a student who is taking a bus to a destination.

CONCLUDING WORDS

Negotiating and teaching in the complex and often confusing landscape of the public schools can sometimes be a daunting process. This book has been written with the desire to provide inspiration and encouragement as well as some structure and practical guidelines for the organization and execution of the O&M specialist's job in a fluid and changeable setting.

I have attempted to bridge the gap between theory and the reality of professional practice with suggestions, strategies, and practical guidelines, running the gamut from forms that help organize a typical school year to strategies for preparing to meet the unforeseeable. Through it all, I have tried to stress that despite diverse challenges, by keeping an open mind, attending to the unique needs and situation of each individual child, and looking for creative solutions in every situation, surviving *and* thriving during a school year is not only possible, but stimulating, gratifying, and rewarding.

References

Anthony, T. L. (2000). Performing a functional low vision assessment. In F. M. D'Andrea & C. Farrenkopf (Eds.), *Looking to learn: Promoting literacy for students with low vision* (pp. 32–73). New York: AFB Press.

Corn, A. L., & Rosenblum, P. L. (2000). *Finding wheels: A curriculum for nondrivers with visual impairments for gaining control of transportation needs.* Austin: Pro-Ed.

Crouse, R. J., & Bina, M. J. (1997). The administration of orientation and mobility programs for children and adults. In B. B. Blasch, W. R. Wiener, & R. L. Welsh (Eds.), *Foundations of orientation and mobility* (2nd ed., pp. 646–659). New York: American Foundation for the Blind.

Erin, J. N., & Paul, B. (1996). Functional vision assessment and instruction of children and youths in academic programs. In A. L. Corn & A. J. Koenig (Eds.), *Foundations of low vision: Clinical and functional perspectives* (pp. 185–220). New York: AFB Press.

Farmer, L. W., & Smith, D. L. (1977). Adaptive technology. In B. B. Blasch, W. R. Wiener, & R. L. Welsh (Eds.), *Foundations of orientation and mobility* (2nd ed., pp. 231–259). New York: American Foundation for the Blind.

Fazzi, D. L., & Petersmeyer, B. A. (2001). *Imagining the possibilities: Creative approaches to orientation and mobility for persons who are visually impaired.* New York: AFB Press.

Guth, D. A., & Rieser, J. J. (1997). Perception and the control of locomotion by blind and visually impaired pedestrians. In B. B. Blasch, W. R. Wiener, & R. L. Welsh (Eds.), *Foundations of orientation and mobility* (2nd ed., pp. 9–38). New York: American Foundation for the Blind.

Hill, E., & Ponder, P. (1976). *Orientation and mobility techniques: A guide to the practitioner.* New York: American Foundation for the Blind.

Hull, J. M. (1990). *Touching the rock: An experience of blindness.* New York: Pantheon Books.

Kapperman, G., Heinze, T., & Sticken, J. (2000). Mathematics. In Koenig, A. J., & Holbrook, M. C. (Eds.), *Foundations of education: Volume 2: Instructional strategies for teaching children and youths with visual impairments* (2nd ed., pp. 370–399). New York: AFB Press.

Koenig, A. J., & Holbrook, M. C. (Eds.). (2000). *Foundations of education: Volume 2: Instructional strategies for teaching children and youths with visual impairments* (2nd ed.). New York: AFB Press.

Koenig, A. J., Holbrook, M. C., Corn, A. L., DePriest, L. B., Erin, J. N., & Presley, I. (2000). Specialized assessments for students with visual impairments. In A. J. Koenig & M. C. Holbrook (Eds.), *Foundations of education, Volume 2. Instructional strategies for teaching children and youths with visual impairments* (2nd ed., pp. 103–153). New York: AFB Press.

Langer, E. J. (1989). *Mindfulness.* Boston: Addison Wesley. As quoted in *Prevention* (March 1991), p. 51.

Marsh, R. A., Hartmeister, F., & Griffin-Shirley, N. (2000). Legal issues for orientation and mobility specialists: Minimizing the risks of liability. *Journal of Visual Impairment & Blindness, 96,* 495–508.

Milian, M., & Erin, J. (Eds.). (2001). *Diversity and visual impairment: The influence of race, gender, religion and ethnicity on the individual.* New York: AFB Press.

Office of Special Education and Rehabilitative Services, U.S. Department of Education. (2000, June 8). Educating blind and visually impaired students: Policy guidance [On-line]. Available at http://www.ed.gov/legislation/FedRegister/other/2000–2/060800a.html

Pogrund, R., Healy, G., Jones, K., Levack, N., Martin-Curry, S., Martinez, C., Marz, J., Roberson-Smith, B., & Vrba, A. (1995). *TAPS: Teaching age-appropriate, purposeful skills: An orientation & mobility curriculum for students with visual impairments* (2nd ed.). Austin: Texas School for the Blind and Visually Impaired.

Pugh, G. S., & Erin, J. (Eds.). (1999). *Blind and visually impaired students: Educational service guidelines.* Watertown, MA: Perkins School for the Blind.

Rowland, C., & Schweigert, P., (2000). *Tangible symbol systems* (2nd ed.). Portland: Oregon Health Sciences University.

Resources

This section contains a sampling of the organizations, companies, publications, and on-line resources that provide invaluable sources of information and products for O&M instructors. For more exhaustive listings, consult the *AFB Directory of Services for Blind and Visually Impaired Persons in the United States and Canada*, published by AFB Press of the American Foundation for the Blind, or AFB's web site, www.afb.org.

SOURCES OF ASSESSMENT TOOLS AND CURRICULA

O&M instructors need to use a variety of assessment tools, depending on their students. The published tools, references, and curricula listed here are widely used in the field. Although some of them are no longer in print, these valuable resources can be found in university libraries.

Brown, D., Simmons, V., Methvin, J., Anderson, S., Boignon, S., & Davis, K. (1991). *Oregon project for visually impaired and blind preschoolers*, (rev. ed.). Medford, OR: Jackson County Education Service District.

An assessment instrument and curriculum designed for young children from birth to age 6 who are blind or visually impaired.

Costello, K. B., Pinkney, P., & Scheffers, W. (1980). *Visual functioning assessment tool*. Chicago: Stoelting.

An assessment that includes sections for evaluating a student's sensory functioning and knowledge of concepts.

Cratty, B. J., Sams, T. A. (1968). Appendix B. In *The body image of blind children.* New York: American Foundation for the Blind.

An assessment addressing a student's ability to identify body parts and body planes and to perform various body movements, including concepts of laterality and directionality.

Dodson-Burk, B., & Hill, E. W. (1989). *Preschool orientation and mobility screening.* Alexandria, VA: Association for Education and Rehabilitation of the Blind and Visually Impaired.

A screening tool that provides a framework for targeting and recording observational and anecdotal information reflecting a child's current level of performing basic O&M skills.

Harley, R. K., Wood, T. A., & Merbler, J. B. (Eds.). (1989). *Peabody mobility kit for infants and toddlers.* Wood Dale, IL: Stoelting.

This kit includes assessment and intervention materials for teachers and parents of children who are visually impaired and have additional disabilities, to promote the development of functional movement and related skills.

Joffee, E. (1999). Approaches to teaching orientation and mobility. In K. M. Huebner, J. G. Prickett, T. R. Welch, & E. Joffee (Eds.). *Hand in hand: Essentials of communication and orientation and mobility for your students who are deaf-blind* (pp. 575-614*).* New York: AFB Press.

The Orientation and Mobility Assessment Fact Sheet contained in this chapter (with a blank copy in the book's appendix) presents a format for recording observations of the student's knowledge and abilities relative to O&M.

Hill, E. W. (1981). *The Hill performance test of selected positional concepts.* Wood Dale, IL: Stoelting.

An individually administered test designed to assess specific positional concepts with children aged 6-10 who are blind or visually impaired.

Pogrund, R., Healy, G., Jones, K., Levack, N., Martin-Curry, S., Martinez, C., Marz, J., Roberson-Smith, B., & Vrba, A. (1995). *Teaching age appropriate skills: An orientation and mobility curriculum for students with visual impairments* (2nd ed.). Austin: Texas School for the Blind and Visually Impaired.

A curriculum providing a collection of ideas and teaching strategies for use by O&M specialists with students aged 3-21 years. Includes assessment materials and a section on adaptive mobility devices with diagrams and directions for assembly.

Specialized skills for the visually handicapped: An instructional manual. (1990). Los Angeles: Frances Blend School, Los Angeles Unified School District.

Assessment inventories and sequences of objectives and skills for students who are visually impaired or blind, from preschool through grade 12. The O&M section provides a skills sequence that may be modified for use with students who are totally blind, have low vision, or have multiple impairments.

BASIC O&M REFERENCES

Blasch, B. B., Wiener, W. R., & Welsh, R. L. (Eds.). (1997). *Foundations of orientation and mobility* (2nd ed.). New York: AFB Press.

A basic O&M textbook and reference covering all the fundamentals.

Fazzi, D. L., & Petersmeyer, B. A. (2001). *Imagining the possibilities: Creative approaches to orientation and mobility for persons who are visually impaired.* New York: AFB Press.

A guide to creative and motivating approaches to teaching O&M.

Hill, E., & Ponder, P. (1976). *Orientation and mobility techniques: A guide for the practitioner.* New York: American Foundation for the Blind.

An O&M techniques manual for the person who is studying to become an O&M specialist and for the certified practitioner.

Levack, N., & Miller, C. (1997). *A paraprofessional's handbook for working with students who are visually impaired.* Austin: Texas School for the Blind and Visually Impaired.

A resource that can be used when working with paraprofessionals. It contains a chapter that defines O&M and the paraprofessional's role.

NATIONAL ORGANIZATIONS

The organizations listed in this section are sources of information and referrals and support for O&M professionals. They hold national conferences, publish books and journals, and serve as advocates for people who are visually impaired.

American Foundation for the Blind
11 Penn Plaza, Suite 300
New York, NY 10001
Phone: (212) 502-7600, (212) 502-7662 (TTY/TDD), (800) AFB-LINE
fax: (212) 502-7777
E-mail: afbinfo@afb.net
Web site: www.afb.org

Provides services to and acts as an information clearinghouse for people who are visually impaired and their families, professionals, organizations, schools, and corporations. Operates the National Technology Center and Career Connect, formerly the Careers and Technology Information Bank; stimulates research and mounts program initiatives to improve services to visually impaired persons; advocates for services and legislation; and maintains the M. C. Migel Library and Information Center. Publishes a wide variety of books, pamphlets, and videos for students, professionals, and researchers; for people involved in making the mainstream community accessible; and for blind and visually impaired people and their families, including the *Directory of Services for Blind and Visually Impaired Persons in the United States and Canada*, the *Journal of Visual Impairment & Blindness*, and *AccessWorld*.

Association for Education and Rehabilitation of the Blind and Visually Impaired
4600 Duke Street, Suite 430
P.O. Box 22397
Alexandria, VA 22304
Phone: (703) 823-9690

fax: (703) 823-9695
E-mail: aernet@laser.net
Web site: www.aerbvi.org

Serves as the membership organization for professionals who are interested in the promotion, development, and improvement of all phases of education and rehabilitation of blind and visually impaired children and adults. Promotes all phases of education and work for people of all ages who are blind or visually impaired, strives to expand their opportunities to take a contributory place in society, and disseminates information. Subgroups include Division 9, Orientation and Mobility (www.aerbvi.org/Division 9). Publishes *RE:view, AER Report,* and *Job Exchange Monthly.*

Council for Exceptional Children
Division on Visual Impairment
1110 North Glebe Road; Suite 300
Arlington, VA 22201-5704
Phone: (703) 620-3660, (888) CEC-SPED, (703) 264-9446 (TTY)
fax: (703) 264-9494
Web site: http://www.cec.sped.org

The largest international professional organization for individuals serving children with disabilities and children who are gifted. Primary activities include advocating for appropriate governmental policies, setting professional standards, providing continuing professional development, and assisting professionals to obtain conditions and resources necessary for effective professional practice. Publishes numerous related materials, journals, and newsletters.

ON-LINE RESOURCES

The Internet is an increasingly effective way to obtain information, keep in contact with colleagues, and keep abreast of issues in the field. Discussion groups do come and go, however, and it is sometimes difficult to determine the reliability of information found on the Internet.

Electronic Discussion Group

Oandm@msu.edu: a list for discussion of topics related to O&M. To subscribe, send an e-mail to listserv@msu.edu and include in the body of the message: subscribe oandm <firstname>< lastname>

Web Sites

Blindness-Related Resources on the Web and Beyond
http://www.hicom.net/~oedipus/blind.html

Blind Links
http://welcome.to/blindlinks

V.I. Guide: A Parent's Guide to Internet Resources about Visual Impairments
http://www.viguide.com

SOURCES OF EQUIPMENT AND MATERIALS

The companies and organizations listed in this section are a sampling of those that provide a variety of products that will be useful to O&M specialists.

3-M Company
3M Center
Building 225-5S.-08
St. Paul, MN 55144-1000
Phone: (612) 733-1110

Supplies Scotchlite reflective sheets that can be used on canes or clothing to make them more visible.

Ambutech
34 DeBaets Street
Winnipeg, Canada R2J 3S9
Phone: (204) 663-3340 or (800) 561-3340
fax: (204) 663-9345
Web site: www.ambutec.com

Supplies a wide variety of canes and accessories, including a large array of cane tips.

American Printing House for the Blind
P.O. Box 6085
1839 Frankfort Avenue
Louisville, KY 40206

Phone: (502) 895-2405 or (800) 223-1839
fax: (502) 895-1509
Web site: http://www.aph.org

Markets instructional aids, tools, and supplies, including the Chang Kit; Picture Maker: Wheatley Tactile Diagram Kit; and Quick-Draw Paper, all of which are useful in producing tactile materials and images.

Autofold, Inc.
P.O. Box 1063
208 Coleman Street
Gardner, MA 01440-1063
Phone: (508) 632-0667
fax: (508) 630-3303
Web site: http://www.autofold.com

Sells a variety of canes.

Corning Medical Optics
Houghton Park
C Building
Corning, NY 14831
Phone: (607) 974-8107
fax: (607) 974-8107
Web site: http://www.corning.com/ophthalmic/glass/cons/
     medical_c_info.html

A source of prescribed eyeglasses for people who have photophobia (light sensitivity). Different filter levels are available.

Exceptional Teaching Aids
20102 Woodbine Avenue
Castro Valley, CA 94546-4232
Phone: (800) 549-6999
fax: (510) 582-5911
Web site: www.exceptionalteaching.com

Provides educational materials for students who are blind or visually impaired, including the Sounder (a wireless doorbell with transmitter and receiver), a teaching tool that can be used in a variety of ways to lead a student toward independence. It also carries survival signs and road signs.

HandiWorks Products for the Blind
10323 Glenoaks Boulevard
Pacoima, CA 91331
Phone: (800) 331-6123
fax: (818) 890-1678
Web site: http://www.handiworks.com

Sells organizational and travel accessories for people who are visually impaired or blind, including a folding cane hip holster, organizing handbags and wallets, and fanny packs.

Innovative Rehabilitation Technology
13467 Colfax Highway
Grass Valley, CA 95945
Phone: (800) 322-4784
fax: (530) 274-2093
Web site: http://www.irti.net

Carries the Wide Angle Mobility Light, canes, and talking and braille compasses, among many other products.

LS & S Group
P.O. Box 673
Northbrook , IL 60065
Phone: (800) 468-4789
fax: (708) 498-1482
Web site: http://www.lssgrp.com

Sells low vision products and canes.

Maxi-Aids
42 Executive Boulevard
P.O. Box 3209
Farmingdale, NY 11735
Phone: (800) 522-6294
fax: (516) 752-0689
Web site: http://www.maxiaids.com

Supplies canes, cane tips, and adaptive aids and devices.

National Federation of the Blind
1800 Johnson Street
Baltimore, MD 21230
Phone: (410) 659-9314
fax: (410) 685-5653
Web site: http://www.nfb.org

A national membership organization for people who are blind that also sells a variety of canes (including fiberglass) and cane tips.

NoIR Medical Technologies
P.O. Box 159
South Lyon, MI 48178
Phone: (734) 769-5565, (800) 521-9746
fax: (734) 769-1708
Web site: www.noir-medical.com

Manufactures sunglasses with chemical absorbers to control the amount of light that passes through them. Some include top and side shields.

Revolution Enterprises
12170 Dearborn Place
Poway, CA 92064
Phone: (800) 382-5132
fax: (619) 679-5788
Web site: www.advantagecanes.com

Sells a line of Advantage canes, including folding and rigid graphite canes with a variety of tips.

Sun Precautions
2815 Wetmore Avenue
Everett, WA 98201
Phone: (800) 882-7860
Fax: (425) 303-0836
Web site: http://www.sunprecautions.com

Offers many items for protection from the sun including SPF 30+ sun-protective clothing, hats, gloves, parasols, sun screens, and sunglasses.

Texas School for the Blind and Visually Impaired
1100 West 45th Street
Austin, TX 78756-3494
Phone: (512) 206-9215
Fax: (512) 206-9452
Web site: http://www.tsvbi.edu

The school offers a variety of publications written by practicing professionals who work with students who are visually impaired or blind, including *TAPS: An Orientation and Mobility Curriculum.*

White Cane Instruments for the Blind
Route 3
P.O. Box 89A
Jenkins, MO 65605
Phone: (417) 574-6368

Sells a variety of canes and cane tips.

Wurzburger Mobility Aids
3900 Cottonwood Drive
Poway, CA 92064
Phone: (510) 682-4585

A source for marshmallow cane tips.

APPENDIX
Checklist of O&M Instructional Areas and Related Objectives

This checklist is a basic planning resource that can be used for noting a student's abilities and targeting potential areas for instruction. It may also be used in writing IEP goals and objectives. It can be expanded and adapted to the individual student and coordinated with assessment findings and developmental and other checklists. It is written in abbreviated form and is not arranged in a necessary sequence.

For detailed objectives for students in wheelchairs, see Orientation and Mobility Assessment for Students with Low Vision in Wheelchairs and Community O&M Assessment and Point Chart for Wheelchair Users in Chapter 8.

BODY IMAGE

☐ identifies/touches own body parts

☐ demonstrates ability to name body parts on self, others, dolls, pictures

☐ identifies function of body parts

☐ identifies right and left parts on self

☐ demonstrates ability to position right or left parts of self near objects

☐ demonstrates ability to position objects to right and left of self

☐ identifies right and left sides of other people and objects

☐ identifies body planes

☐ identifies relationships of body parts

☐ identifies relationships of objects to body

☐ identifies relationships of body to objects

BODY MOVEMENT

☐ demonstrates independent movement

☐ demonstrates correct body posture

☐ demonstrates ability to execute measured turns: eighth, quarter, half, full

☐ demonstrates various gaits: walk, hop, skip, run, and so on

☐ demonstrates various movements: crawling, squatting, bending, stamping, and the like

☐ demonstrates ball-handling skills

☐ demonstrates body conditioning/strength building with or without weights

☐ demonstrates relaxation techniques

SENSORY SKILLS

Kinesthetic and Proprioceptive

☐ identifies position of body parts

☐ identifies inclines/declines, slopes: forward, right, left

Tactile

☐ identifies various textures with hands and feet

☐ identifies qualities of materials: wet/dry, solid/compressible, and so on

☐ identifies comparative temperatures

☐ identifies comparative thickness

☐ identifies comparative depth

☐ demonstrates reduction in tactile defensiveness

☐ demonstrates ability to use tactile cues/clues

Olfactory

☐ identifies various smells associated with different places

☐ demonstrates ability to use olfactory clues

Visual

☐ identifies visual clues, for example, when lacks depth perception or has a field loss

☐ demonstrates ability to use low vision aids: CCTV, magnifier, monocular/binoculars (to locate stationary and locate/track moving targets)

☐ demonstrates ability to use sunware

☐ demonstrates use of patterned scanning techniques

Auditory

☐ identifies environmental sounds

☐ demonstrates ability to localize sound

☐ demonstrates ability to follow verbal, taped directions

☐ demonstrates ability to use sound to orient movement, as when walking parallel to traffic sounds

☐ demonstrates ability to perceive objects and use sense to orient self, as when walking parallel to walls

SPATIAL, QUANTITATIVE, AND TEMPORAL CONCEPTS

☐ demonstrates knowledge of comparative geometric shapes

☐ demonstrates knowledge of directional concepts: up/down, in/out, and so forth

☐ demonstrates knowledge of positional concepts: next to, open/ closed, and the like

☐ demonstrates knowledge of comparative size

☐ demonstrates knowledge of time: minute, hour, day, noon, a.m., evening, and so on

ORIENTING SKILLS

General Orienting Skills

☐ demonstrates ability to seat self: chair, row seating, picnic table, and so forth

☐ demonstrates direction taking ability: perpendicular, parallel, angled

☐ demonstrates ability to identify indoor features: door, handrail, fire extinguisher, and the like

☐ demonstrates ability to familiarize self to room using search patterns: gridline, perimeter

☐ demonstrates ability to identify outdoor features, such as curb, driveways, ramps, and streets

☐ demonstrates ability to identify weather features: wind, air currents, shade, temperature, and so on

☐ demonstrates ability to recover dropped objects using a variety of search patterns

☐ demonstrates ability to use left and right when embedded in directions

☐ demonstrates knowledge/use of units of measurement, including inch, foot, block, and mile

☐ demonstrates ability to estimate measurements

☐ demonstrates knowledge of concepts of parallel and perpendicular

☐ demonstrates ability to use cardinal directions: N, S, E, W; NE, SW, and so forth

☐ demonstrates ability to use compass: print, braille

☐ demonstrates ability to use ordinal directions, including first, second, and third

☐ demonstrates ability to use numbering systems: rooms, streets, addresses, and the like

☐ demonstrates ability to identify street types, for example, one way, two way

☐ demonstrates ability to identify traffic movement, patterns, density

☐ demonstrates knowledge of traffic regulations

☐ demonstrates knowledge of time-distance relationships

☐ demonstrates ability to define orientation and mobility in concrete terms relevant to skill level

Use of Landmarks

☐ demonstrates ability to identify properties of landmarks: stationary, descriptors, and so forth

☐ demonstrates ability to identify landmarks

☐ demonstrates ability to use landmarks

☐ demonstrates ability to sequence/reverse sequence of landmarks

☐ demonstrates ability to choose/sequence own landmarks

Map Skills

☐ demonstrates ability to use visual, tactile, auditory maps

☐ demonstrates ability to create visual, tactile, auditory maps

BASIC SKILLS

Human Guide

☐ demonstrates knowledge of basic human guide skills and variations

☐ demonstrates ability to change directions

☐ demonstrates ability to transfer sides

☐ demonstrates ability to negotiate narrow passageways

☐ demonstrates ability to accept/refuse aid

☐ demonstrates ability to negotiate stairs

☐ demonstrates ability to negotiate doorways

☐ demonstrates ability to negotiate seating

Self-protection

☐ demonstrates upper hand and forearm technique

☐ demonstrates lower arm and forearm technique

☐ demonstrates trailing technique

☐ demonstrates traversing open doors/space; maintaining line of travel

CANE SKILLS

☐ demonstrates ability to name parts of a cane

☐ demonstrates ability to maintain appropriate grip or grips

☐ demonstrates ability to store/retrieve cane

☐ demonstrates ability to use cane holder

☐ demonstrates ability to unfold and fold a folding or telescopic cane

☐ demonstrates ability to control/handle cane selectively with a human guide

☐ demonstrates ability to use diagonal technique

☐ demonstrates ability to clear with cane

☐ demonstrates ability to center cane

☐ demonstrates ability to produce arc with safe coverage

☐ demonstrates ability to maintain rhythm

☐ demonstrates ability to walk in step

☐ demonstrates ability to use constant contact technique

☐ demonstrates ability to use touch technique

☐ demonstrates ability to use verification technique

☐ demonstrates ability to trail: diagonal/touch techniques

☐ demonstrates ability to use cane selectively

☐ demonstrates ability to use cane for identification purposes

☐ demonstrates ability to use cane to detect obstacles

☐ demonstrates ability to use cane to detect drop-offs

☐ demonstrates ability to use cane to negotiate obstacles without losing line of direction

☐ demonstrates ability to perform a straight line of travel

☐ demonstrates ability to use cane to ascend/descend stairs

☐ demonstrates ability to use cane to examine objects

☐ demonstrates ability to use cane to detect/negotiate changes in terrain

☐ demonstrates ability to use cane to trail a shoreline

☐ demonstrates ability to use touch and drag technique

☐ demonstrates ability to use touch and slide technique

☐ demonstrates ability to use three-point technique

☐ demonstrates ability to alternate techniques as situation warrants

☐ demonstrates ability to use cane for street-crossing preparation

☐ demonstrates ability to use cane to exit street

COMMUNITY TRAVEL SKILLS

Vehicle Negotiation/Passenger Skills

☐ demonstrates ability to differentiate front of vehicle from back

☐ demonstrates ability to identify passenger and driver sides

☐ demonstrates ability to differentiate front and back doors/seats

☐ demonstrates ability to store/retrieve cane outside a vehicle to free hands

☐ demonstrates ability to open, lock, and close a door from the outside

☐ demonstrates ability to seat self and store cane inside

☐ demonstrates ability to fasten and unfasten seat belt

☐ demonstrates ability to close, lock, and unlock a door from the inside

☐ demonstrates ability to use vehicle visor to shield face from sun when needed

☐ demonstrates ability to define/explain disabled parking permit concepts, privileges, and laws

☐ demonstrates ability to place and remove disabled parking placard within vehicle

Personal Information

☐ demonstrates knowledge of personal information, such as name, address, and phone number

☐ demonstrates knowledge of critical information about self, including visual impairment and medical and related conditions

Street Crossing

☐ demonstrates knowledge of pedestrian/traffic rules, regulations, laws

☐ demonstrates ability to identify street corners

☐ demonstrates ability to align self for crossing

☐ demonstrates ability to identify sound-masking situations

☐ demonstrates ability to identify sound shadow situations

☐ demonstrates ability to identify type of intersection

☐ demonstrates ability to identify intersection controls and the lack thereof

☐ demonstrates ability to locate and use pedestrian traffic controls

☐ demonstrates ability to identify traffic patterns

☐ demonstrates ability to use silence as the main clue for timing crossing

☐ demonstrates ability to use sound of perpendicular/parallel traffic as the main clue for timing crossing

☐ demonstrates ability to perform patterned scanning before and during crossing

☐ demonstrates ability to determine if potential crossing is unsafe without assistance

☐ demonstrates ability to solicit aid for street crossing

☐ demonstrates ability to perform street-crossing recovery

Shopping Skills

☐ demonstrates ability to identify/organize money

☐ demonstrates ability to store/retrieve money in wallet, pocket, purse, or fanny pack

☐ demonstrates ability to locate entrance/exit of store

☐ demonstrates ability to solicit aid for locating items/departments

☐ demonstrates ability to use shopping service if necessary

☐ demonstrates ability to produce and/or use shopping list

☐ demonstrates ability to locate departments, items

☐ demonstrates ability to use monocular to read store directories/ department labels

☐ demonstrates ability to use shopping basket/cart

☐ demonstrates ability to locate cashier/open checkout stand

☐ demonstrates ability to travel through line

☐ demonstrates ability to make purchase

Public Transportation Skills

☐ demonstrates ability to plan trip by phoning transit company/using transit schedules

☐ demonstrates ability to locate bus stop

☐ demonstrates ability to enter/exit bus

☐ demonstrates ability to locate appropriate seat

☐ demonstrates ability to identify/solicit aid to identify destination bus stop

☐ demonstrates ability to conduct transfer

MISCELLANEOUS SKILLS

☐ demonstrates ability to identify self as someone who is blind or visually impaired

☐ demonstrates ability to name and explain the cause and effect of own visual impairment/blindness

☐ demonstrates ability to use elevator

☐ demonstrates ability to use escalator

☐ demonstrates ability to use pay phone

☐ demonstrates ability to dial 911

☐ demonstrates ability to obtain DMV identification card

Index

About the Author

Natalie Isaak Knott , M.A., is an Orientation and Mobility Specialist and a Teacher of Students with Visual Impairment in the West Contra Costa Unified School District in Richmond, California. A dedicated teacher for more than 25 years, master teacher to O&M student teachers, and mentor to many other first-time teachers, she has particularly focused on students with multiple disabilities. She has contributed to *Long Cane News* and presented her work at the California Orientation and Mobility Specialists conference.

CPSIA information can be obtained
at www.ICGtesting.com
Printed in the USA
LVOW03s1512180316
479779LV00003B/56/P